Oklahoma Tenor

Oklahoma Tenor

Musical Memories of Giuseppe Bentonelli

by JOSEPH BENTON

Foreword by Eva Turner
Introduction by B. A. Nugent

UNIVERSITY OF OKLAHOMA PRESS : NORMAN

San Francisco Public Library

3 1223 00323 5729

Copyright 1973 by the University of Oklahoma Press, Publishing Division of the University. Composed and printed at Norman, Oklahoma, U.S.A., by the University of Oklahoma Press. First edition.

Foreword

When I was asked to write a foreword to this book by my dear and valued friend, Joseph Benton, the thought immediately came to my mind of how much I owe him for one of the most delightful and treasured epochs of my own life, for it was his suggestion that I should come to Norman in 1949 as a visiting Professor of Voice for a period of nine months. This eventually turned out to be a decade, for I stayed, not for nine months but for ten years! And what a happy ten years that was.

Although I had known Joseph since 1929 (I first met him as Giuseppe Bentonelli at The Arena of Verona, Italy, when we were singing there in the same season), the time in Oklahoma gave me the opportunity to know him much better and to revel with him in the nostalgic journeys of our respective careers and I have always found him a kind man and a loyal friend.

This collection of delightful and amusing anecdotes is a book which, I feel sure, will have the effect on the reader of revitalising dampened spirits and unfurrowing the most troubled brow!

Vivat Giuseppe!

Eva Turner

Introduction

Joseph Benton's truly delightful stories are collected here under a most appropriate title, *Oklahoma Tenor*. This world-famous tenor from the Sooner State once again shares with his listeners his art, blended with human values, told in his own unique style with mellifluous charm, and garnished with the proud heritage of his homeland.

For Joseph Benton always belonged to Oklahoma. He grew up there. He now resides there, where his lodgement extends to a permanent niche in The Oklahoma Hall of Fame. In between, as Giuseppe Bentonelli, he thrilled audiences the world over in Italy, France, Sicily, Belgium, Holland, Egypt, and Yugoslavia, as well as across the United States and Canada, from the Metropolitan Opera to Chicago to the Hollywood Bowl. Millions of others, not privileged to hear him in person, enjoyed his performances over network radio and via his recordings. His stage colleagues included the likes of John Charles Thomas, Leonard Warren, Ezio Pinza, Lily Pons, Rosetta Pampanini, Lawrence Tibbett,

Gina Cigna, Carmen Melis, Claudia Muzio, Georges Baklanoff, Lucrezia Bori, Vina Bovy, Teiko Kiva, and Edith Mason.

As Giuseppe Bentonelli, he was the first major American artist to reach the operatic meridian in Europe, where, by adopting the Italian version of his name, he was accepted as one of their own. They loved him all the more for his many humanitarian deeds, and for the manner in which he accepted them. To be sure, they adopted him with almost parental affection and pride as they watched his career grow. In 1934, Giuseppe Bentonelli was chosen as one of the four most popular operatic tenors singing in Italy.

Joseph Horace Benton was born in Kansas City, Missouri, the middle of three sons born to Oliver Horace and Ada LaMiza Seawell Benton. He quickly became an Oklahoman when, at age two, his parents moved to Sayre, Oklahoma (then known as Riverton), where he spent his boyhood. From the University of Oklahoma he received three degrees: a Bachelor of Arts in Spanish and French (1920), a Bachelor of Music in Voice (1921), and a Master of Arts in Modern Languages—Italian and French (1941). At the University, he also earned membership in Phi Beta Kappa.

In 1923, Joseph Benton established residency in Nice, France, where he studied voice under the world-renowned teacher, Jean de Reszke. In Nice, he made his European debut in Mozart's *Don Giovanni*. From 1925 through 1928, he studied opera scores, Italian, and diction in Milan, Italy, with Maestro Vittorio Vanzo, who, as principal conductor at La Scala, had introduced Wagner's operas to Italy only a few years previous. On February 4, 1928, with Maestro Vanzo in the audience at Faenza, near Bologna, Giuseppe Bentonelli made his debut in Italy in Verdi's *La Traviata*. This successful debut was followed by more than five hundred performances during important opera seasons throughout Europe, Africa, and the United States. Giuseppe Bentonelli, the leading tenor from Oklahoma, soon became a household word among opera connoisseurs on three continents.

As Giuseppe Bentonelli, he created leading tenor roles in two operas at their world premieres: Antonio Smareglia's *The Vassal* at Trieste (1930) and Licinio Refice's *Cecilia* at the Royal Opera House in Rome (1934). In 1935, he sang the leading tenor role in the American premiere of Ottorino Respighi's *The Flame* at the Opera of Chicago, along with a cast which included Rosa Raisa and Giacomo Rimini, with Richard Hageman conducting.

In 1934, Joseph Benton returned to the United States where, with Maria Jeritza, Pasquale Amato, and Maestro Gennaro Papi, he made his American debut at the Opera of Chicago in a performance of *Tosca* by Giacomo Puccini. That Chicago also warmly received him is evidenced by the fact that he sang forty-nine performances of seventeen different operas there until financial woes forced the closing of this famous company.

In January of 1936, Giuseppe Bentonelli made his debut with the Metropolitan Opera alongside Lucrezia Bori in a performance of Jules Massenet's *Manon*. He subsequently appeared in seventeen performances of six operas at the Met. There followed also several years of extensive tours across the United States and Canada as a member of the Metropolitan Opera Quartet.

To the good fortune of his many students, his many friends, and his family, Joseph Benton returned to the University of Oklahoma in 1944, where he served as Professor of Music until retirement in 1969.

B. A. Nugent

This book, then, offers a treasure chest of recollections, anecdotal, informative, and entertaining to the reader. This book has given me the pleasure of knowing Joseph Benton, our *Oklahoma Tenor*, not briefly since our introduction in 1971, but for many, many rewarding years.

B. A. Nugent

Norman, Oklahoma

Table of Contents

Foreword, by Eva Turner v
Introduction, by B. A. Nugent vii
Things Divine (a sonnet) 2
The Hückel Hat 3
Needless Fears (a sonnet) 8
Those French Recitatives Sung in Italian! 9
The Night That Faust Lost His Tights on Stage 15
Memories (a sonnet) 20
Catholics and Presbyterians 21
Morning 26
The Darda Portrait 27
Maestro Vittorio Maria Vanzo 29
Evening 34
Regarding Ernestine Schumann-Heink 35
The Quiet Sea 38
Amelita Galli-Curci 39

Ostend and the Locked-in Keys 45
Our Opera Season in Tripoli 49
The Oratorio "Moses" at Treviso 55
The Arena of Verona 59
Leading Role in a World Premiere 83
Royal Opera of Cairo 87
The Little, Old, Gray Home 94
Knowing Jean de Reszke 95
Love Was a Little Thing 100
The Assuan Dam, 1931 101
Spirit's Retrospect 106
The Rolex 107
Warning 110
A Hug from Tosca 111
Stale Fish in Venice 115
Tuna Fish in a Can 119
Sicilian Interlude 123
The Cycle 128
Up One Minute, Down the Next 129
First Plane Ride 133
Opera in English Radio Hour 137
Erna Sack 139
The Protested Tenor 141
Diplomatic Dinner 143
Iphigenia in Aulis 145
Will Rogers 147
Why 150

List of Illustrations

Joseph Benton 67
As the Duke in Verdi's *Rigoletto* 68
As Rodolfo in Puccini's *La Bohème* 69
As Pinkerton in Puccini's *Madama Butterfly* 70
As photographed for the New York *Times* 71
As Roméo in Gounod's *Roméo et Juliette* 72
As Julien in *Louise* 73
As Jenik in Smetana's *The Bartered Bride* 74
In Massenet's *Manon* 75
Sight-seeing in Egypt 76
In Verdi's *La Traviata* 77
As Gerald in *Lakmé* 78
As Lionello in Flotow's *Marta* 79
As Rinuccio in Puccini's *Gianni Schicchi* 80
As Azor in Respighi's *The Flame* 81
Joseph Benton 82

Oklahoma Tenor

Things Divine

When I try to name the things we hold divine,
The simple things of life swarm up to me
And show their strength through calm tranquility,
Like evening hours that bring a peace benign.
Among the things divine which each heart hides
Are: Faith in friends and Hope of happiness,
A future Home with joy of Love's caress,
An open Hearth where quiet Peace abides.

So, as we look into the years that dawn
Far down the misty valley, there we find
The fragrance of the years we've left behind
Which floats across the hills already trod.
This gives us renewed Hope to gaze upon
The impregnable bright battlements of God.

The Hückel Hat

Did you ever have a hankering for something which you did not need but without which you felt out of style, left out, almost ostracized by others with more money than yourself? Such was my emotional state for several weeks after first going to study in Italy and seeing the then-very-stylish Hückel velvet hats being worn by those men-in-the-know in Milan.

I already had a good American Stetson hat but somehow without my having one of those dapper Hückel hoods from Vienna to wear, it seemed that everyone was ostracizing me. Those were the days of Fascism in Italy and most things of foreign extraction were suspect; not so with those Hückel hats from Vienna; they were *the* thing, the final topping which showed the difference between the plebs and the hotsy-totsys. My envy leaped high whenever one came into view, whether on the head of a Milanese man or when viewed through the showcase of a hat shop. But the price prevented my investment; voice lessons were the reason for my being in

Italy and lessons have to be paid for, not to mention the many inescapable financial fringes that surround one's vocal study.

However, one day the temptation was just too great and I fell victim to an "On Sale" sign in a chic hat shop on Via Manzoni, Milan. I entered "just to look at the hat up close," but came out wearing one of the handsome soft black velvet bonnets and carrying my perfectly good but now "old" Stetson in a hat-bag. Then a new problem arose: how was I going to announce the fact of owning a Hückel hat to the family at whose home I lived without their upping the price of my board and room? Two days of trepidation passed. On that second day the radio stations, newspapers, and bull horns mounted on cruising trucks announced the stupendous news that Il Duce, Benito Mussolini, was going to make his first speech in Milan from the steps of the world-famous Cathedral the following evening and that all of Milan's citizens were cordially required to be there to hear him.

"First things first," so that was a chance to inaugurate my Hückel under proper festive auspices. The Lattuada family with whom I lived, partly out of curiosity, partly out of fear of *not* going, announced that they were going to be present for Mussolini's speech and that we would have our evening meal one hour earlier than usual; would that be agreeable? Yes, since I was planning to go, too (eyebrows were raised appropriately). The day came, the hour approached, the early meal was eaten and each of us left the house separately on purpose so that there would be no kick-back criticisms from among neighbors or explanations to be made regarding political beliefs or disbeliefs. (In those days one was not permitted to have any political beliefs other than those in favor of Fascism and its all-powerful leader, Il Duce.)

It was about one and one-half miles from where I lived to

THE HUCKEL HAT

the Piazza del Duomo where Mussolini was to make his speech. I took a tram as far as the tram was permitted by traffic officers to go, then walked the extra blocks and dutifully took a place among the 125,000 (according to the papers) party faithful waiting in the piazza. The entire day, like so many in that wet city of Milan, had been threatening rain and with the coming of evening, the clouds increased their promise of foul weather. Since this was to be a really ("rally") big evening, I had worn my new Hückel hat, partly in honor of the old buzzard's speech, partly because it seemed a good chance to give the new velvet topper an appropriate initiation.

The streets entering the Piazza del Duomo are wide and numerous; from every one of them tens of thousands of people poured themselves into the huge square and by the minute the pressure became more intense. Did you ever stand in a crowd so immense and packed so tightly that only with genuine difficulty could you get your hand to your face? Such was the jam in which I soon found myself. My position in the crowd was quite near to the steps of the great Cathedral from which the old buzzard was going to speak, so I was again pleased that Signora Lattuada had served our evening meal early. The rank smell of garlic and second-hand cheap wine was seemingly on every breath, but other than that, the enormous crowd was orderly. Some of my impacted neighbors were cordial enough to start visiting with their enforced *"à côtés"* and even with me, a foreigner. As the moment for the speech came closer, tighter grew the excitement, some of it feigned, of course, since no one can ever really get sincerely excited about Fascism; however, we Latins are a hot-blooded bunch and never emotionally tepid. No bands were playing, only tension of the explosive type was in the air.

Then, on the tick of the second, the great usually-closed Porta della Gloria, or Glory Door, used only for a visit of the Pope or other dignitary, opened and a bunch of men in uniforms of black shirts and motorcycle-rider pants and boots, came through that door in phalanx formation, the one in the middle being Benito Mussolini, the former Milanese seller of wine-across-the-counter but now head of the "New Order," Il Duce, Leader of Fascism, which was going to change the world "and last one thousand years." A cheer went up like one has never heard and never will hear again; it lasted many minutes. When finally the spoken word could be heard, the microphones blared at throat-and-ear-splitting volume the divine message.

The speech had progressed some four minutes when without warning the weatherman pulled out the bottom of the rain-barrel and before even the edges of that enormous crowd could give room to the others toward its center, everyone was soaked to the marrow. But not even such a deluge could gum up the limpid lip of Mussolini; on and on he went as wetter and wetter we got until saturation could no longer be saturated.

And that Hückel? It was supposed to be of fast-dye but evidently was one of those made in a hurry to supply the great demand for Hückel hats, or perhaps being sold in Italy, it was supposed to be worn only where the sun shines all of the time. But in any case, that new hat literally *melted* and its black dye ran down not only over my face like coffee from an overflowing cup, but even my scalp was black, and the stains on my shirt and underclothing never did wash out. After that hat had completely dried I had it blocked but it never looked right because the soaking had taken all of the sizing out of the brim. This made the brim droop like the ears of a Beagle and even when a new headband was installed, the hat was eternally stretching to too large a size which caused the hat to settle over my ears like a tired towel.

So ends the tale of my first purchase in Italy. It concludes with a paraphrased quotation from the Good Book: "Pride goeth before destruction and a Hückel hat before a fall."

Needless Fears

*Through all the churnings of the toilsome years
There is a hope that is a part of me:
The hope that some day I may chance to see
The closing chapter of our book of fears,
When all the snagging doubts that fill our way
Will be uprooted, piled and later burned
Like seeded weeds; then the ground be turned
And sown to Hope whose roots will last alway.*

*For, idle fears are foolish anyway,
And yet they come and menace each of us
With worryings, if's and and's and needless fuss
That consume and take from us what might have been
The making of a work that would last alway
And take away some harshness from Life's din.*

Those French Recitatives Sung in Italian!

French is an old language. It is bristling with time-weighted proverbs and century-aged folk-stories and old-wives' tales of varying ages; the choice is so changeable, so vast, that one can easily find embarrassing alternatives in those patterns of speech to embellish almost any subject under high heaven. An example of what the average Frenchman thinks of four of the world languages is concentrated into the following, a saying common throughout the land—notice that French comes first:

> *Le francais?—pour l'amour* (French?—for love)
> *L'italien?—pour le chant* (Italian?—for singing)
> *L'anglais?—pour les affairs* (English?—for business)
> *L'allemand?—c'est la langue des chevaux!* (German?—it's the language of horses!)

It is evident from the above final punch-line toward which language the gun is aimed. There is an interplay between the French original and an opera's libretto after it has been translated into Italian. This is almost requisite since very few Italian opera singers know French. (Their singing sounds like it, too.)

There is a clarity about written French that cannot be altered or changed, not even by a calculating attorney-at-law; it means one thing and one thing only. In fact, for long years past and today also whenever a treaty of peace is signed at the termination of a war, the conditions of such treaty are written in each of the languages of the formerly warring countries then translated into French because the angular French language cannot be altered or elasticized into meaning something else—as is an easy possibility with English, especially when in the claws of scheming international lawyers.

One line of the above saying opines that Italian is for singing. How true—even an Italian's speech is musical. The Italian language is found also to some extent in the sciences, especially chemistry, and in the manufacturing of dyes but, like the innuendo regarding the use of German, Italian's most happy employment is accomplished as the text to singing. Since opera is Italy's outstanding contribution to the field of music, we shall confine our remarks to that form of the tonal art.

Jules Massenet, after Gounod, has ever been the most enjoyed composer of French opera and in the United States his operas *Manon*, *Werther*, and *Hérodiade* are on full speaking terms with the operas of both Verdi and Wagner. Few opera-tunes enjoy more popularity than Massenet's "Méditation" from his opera *Thaïs*, not forgetting his "Elegie" from the dramatic work *Erinyes* by Leconte deLisle.

During the years that Benito Mussolini held sway over the political destiny of his native land, there was little sympathy between the various factions of the nation: all foreign-language newspapers were squelched as being subversive and were forced to go out of business; the red-tape regarding foreigners' passports was enormously tightened; and foreign goods, especially machinery made of steel, were curtailed to a minimum. If you were not a member of the Fascist Party then you were a "zero" or a foreigner open to all sorts of personal and political insults and niggardly belittlings, a person suspect because you had not been born somewhere in the Boot of Italy instead of wherever it was that you were born.

It was then that I realized that my career would be a short and thorny one if it continued under the Scotch name of Benton. My teacher of diction, Signorina Sila Conti-Varesi, granddaughter of the famous baritone, Felice Varesi, who created the role of Rigoletto, had lived during her teen-age years in Chicago and understood the psychological spasms that were my daily worry. She had been present at my debut (Alfredo in Verdi's *La Traviata*) which had been made under my own name of Benton. Signorina Varesi suggested (since political pressures were what they were) that I alter my name by adding "elli" to the Anglo-Saxon base and thus appease the black-shirted, steaming-hot young Fascists, each of whom was trying to outdo the other members of his platoon in persecuting foreigners in the name of Il Partito Fascista (The Fascist Party) and Il Duce (The Leader, or Mussolini).

Toward the end of February, 1929, I finished singing *La Bohème* at Modena, Italy, in that city's very beautiful municipal opera house where my Mimì was that unique singing-actress and, later on, the voice teacher of Renata Tebaldi, Signora Carmen Melis. The Ragazzini management from Milan which was coining the money on this season—every standing spot being filled—smelled still more money. Signor Ragazzini conceived the idea of presenting Signora Melis in Mantua where he commanded the opera season that year as well as in Modena. And since Massenet's *Manon* had not been presented there for several seasons but had been under consideration before the season started, he wanted to profit by Signora Melis' fame in the title role of that opera and present her there as a fitting closing to the city's opera season. Signor Ragazzini was always looking for a feather to put into his own personal cap and this time he truly found it in *Manon*. (Ragazzini was a disappointed opera singer himself, properly described as a constipated baritone. But he was so tight financially that he squeezed every lira until it screamed High C.)

In those days of political and financial unrest, transportation was truly awkward. Federally owned railroads were almost as irregular and off-schedule as were the toll-highways with their yawning chuck-holes. The success of the *Manon* Gala with Carmen Melis was truly an artistic event even for Mantua, the locale of the story of Verdi's opera *Rigoletto*. Without the excessive (to Ragazzini) cost of bringing another tenor from Milan, I was the only tenor available, so Ragazzini asked me if I thought myself capable of moving in "high society," operatically, with such luminaries as Carmen Melis. With true Oklahoma bravado, I answered in the affirmative. This was partly because I had had my costumes for *Manon* made in Milan in hopes of getting to do the role. The costumes for the *Manon* tenor are most important. I had studied the role but had never had a chance to perform it.

The final performance of *Bohème* at Modena, which closed the city's hugely successful opera season, was another large success. We got seventeen curtain calls, but excused ourselves early from the party held in our honor afterward to leave by

THOSE FRENCH RECITATIVES

livery car for Mantua that night where on the following evening we were to sing *Manon*. Imagine my sudden chance to sing *Manon* in Italy and in Italian! I had done it in French in France, but the Italian version has recitatives which are sung, not recited; and they are complicated as to language, especially for a foreigner, even one with an Oklahoma accent.

Fortunately we had a good driver and an almost-new Lanza livery car in which to make the overland trip from Modena to Mantua. There had been a snowstorm that day, but the paper that evening had said that the inter-provincial highways were open. It was around midnight when we pulled away from the Hotel Regina in Modena. The first few miles in the hill country were spanned easily; then it began to sleet heavily and before one could realize it, those roads were like glass and our car was sliding about like a cat on a frozen roof, impossible to guide at any but the slowest pace—and even then dangerous. We found ourselves uttering constant silent prayers and exclamations of solar plexus fright. The one thing which made our snow-tires so unstable was that the inside lane of the highway had been banked in that hilly country for safety from speed which now, covered with snow and thick sleet, only added to the slickness and danger of the highway. Thanks to our driver's creeping along at a snail's pace we finally got to Mantua around 4:45 A.M., all in one piece but with our hearts sore from having swallowed them desperately so many times as we drove over that treacherously banked, ice-covered highway.

Having a new tenor demanded an orchestral rehearsal; I was thankful for this help. We rehearsed with the orchestra in the opera house for almost four hours that afternoon (no union demanding its financial rake-off for overtime). Signora Melis was most helpful with suggestions about how to do those sung recitatives. I came to the opera house two hours before the beginning of the performance. All theatrical performances in Italy, no matter what, begin at 9:00 P.M. The bugaboo sung-recitatives with a few exceptions went remarkably well during the performance. In fact, they were like that sleet when the sun shone upon it: they melted into nothingness, and I found myself sailing along like one of the Fascists at a meeting with his peers and native confrères. What a sensation! But I shall always remember that great lady of the operatic stage, Signora Carmen Melis, the sleet-slick highway on which we ran between *La Bohème* and *Manon*, and the dangerous chances we took that sleety night in the late 1920's in Italy.

The Night That Faust Lost His Tights on Stage

My debut in opera in Italy did not take place until three years after my arrival in that country since the language had to be learned as well as a representative list of opera scores memorized in Italian. At that time it was usually necessary for Americans wanting an operatic debut in Italy to pay perfumedly for it through unscrupulous agents operating mysteriously under the tarnished cloak of Fascism, men who were padding their personal wallets at the expense of gullible Americans. And once you had paid for your initial debut, you had to do likewise for subsequent engagements as well. It was a vicious circle with a repeated chorus of "Pay, Pay, Pay."

Various agents had approached me privately wanting to "provide" me a debut in opera in Italy, but when finances were discussed these agents said that an "initial remuneration" would be expected for themselves. However, they never got around to quoting precisely how much or any of the other important details, so I thanked each one and proceeded to study as though we had not even spoken together, hoping against hope that one of them would one day find himself in a jam and that such would be the break for which I had been hoping and studying. Such never became fact, however.

In the fall of 1927 Signor Manlio Pasotto, a reputable agent who had his own office in downtown Milan, contacted me through an Italian baritone who was a mutual acquaintance, and said that the following February he would be presenting several performances of three operas at Faenza, Italy. (Faenza is an ancient city near Bologna and famous for its ceramics; the French noun *faïence* comes from the name of this city whose crackled-design ceramics have been famous for centuries.) Pasotto said that he was willing to give me a debut in the unthankful role of Alfredo in Verdi's *La Traviata* provided I would be willing to appear at a near-nothing price.

I thought the proposition over, agreed to take a chance, and we signed the contract, a huge document in those days of Mussolini-ridden Italy, filled with more curious demands than a wartime questionnaire. It demanded one's "party affiliations," duplicates of one's "career as a party-member," and answers to such impertinent questions as "for how long have you been a Fascist?," "name of next of kin to be notified should you not return from a party assignment." All of this had to be filled out in quintuplicate, each copy with its own fee, then filed with proper notarizations at the Office of the Fascist Syndicate in Milan. One copy deposited with the Milan police and the original copy sent by registered mail to the head Opera Office in Rome; the other two copies were for those who were agreeing to the original contract. With all the weight of useless detail which was required those days under the yoke of Fascism, it is remarkable that anyone ever got anything done.

FAUST LOST HIS TIGHTS

The debut in *La Traviata* took place and the repeat performances as well, in the pretty, old-timish opera house of Faenza. They were risingly successful and my noted coach, Maestro Vittorio Vanzo, came from Milan to my debut performance. The municipally sponsored opera season there that year had begun with Gounod's *Faust* and was closing four weeks later with Verdi's *La Traviata*. In between these two operas, Verdi's *Il Trovatore* had been given, all of them for a total of nineteen performances. The handsome old opera house was jammed at each performance and dark only on Tuesday nights as such was the "day of rest" then in Italy. The tenor who had already done six performances of the title role of *Faust* was extremely fatigued from having sung that opera already four times during the final week, so when Signor Pasotto vaguely suggested that it might be arranged for me to sing the final performance of *Faust* and let the weary tenor return to Milan following the next-to-last giving of the opera, I jumped at the chance.

As a matter of truth it must be said that Signor Pasotto had paid me the sum agreed upon in the contract for each of the *La Traviata* performances. For this unexpected *Faust*, however, I agreed to sing gratis—it is ever very difficult to put an opera into one's repertoire even now under the most favorable conditions and in one's own country. Hoping that such a break as my getting to sing *Faust* might occur, weeks earlier I had had my costumes for *Faust* made in Milan before leaving for Faenza to sing *La Traviata*. And very handsome costumes they were, too. I telephoned the costumer, he sent them by express and I wore them proudly. Doing two operas and both for the first time anywhere during one's debut-season was certainly a bonanza enjoyed by few young hopefuls in those days. Little did I think when donning this stage finery what was going to happen to it and me that same night.

The story of the opera *Faust* requires a rapid change of costumes on the darkened stage in the Prologue to Act I, when Satan, in exchange for the soul of the aged Faust, gives him renewed youth and changes him into a dashing young cavalier. The tenor must wear the young man's finery under the scholastic robe and old man's wig in which the old Faust appears in the Prologue; and it seemed to me that if tights take the place of pants, tights also should be held up by suspenders (braces). So I wore the fine evening galluses bought at Marshall Field's store in Chicago on my way to Europe but which up to then had been kept to wear exclusively with my evening clothes. The pairs of tights for each of my two changes being brand-new, I had had the housekeeper at my hotel in Milan sew six suspender buttons on each of the tights; but not until later did I know why she had smiled so questioningly while doing this requested service.

The tricky change from the old to the young Faust was accomplished without bobble as to time limit, and with much applause the Prologue had closed. The Garden Scene went well, too, especially the acting. The soprano singing the role of Marguerite was that famous lady of Italian opera, Carmen Melis, who had sung the first performance anywhere of Puccini's *Girl of the Golden West* (in Boston). Signora Melis' acting was notable even when judged by dramatic standards. She had suggested during the run-through, which the management begrudgingly had accorded me, some by-play which would fill in the several pages of orchestral postlude to the Garden Scene and thus make more believable the closing of this act, certainly more convincing than ending it with the usual clinch-and-kiss lasting minutes.

That night I felt well, knew that my costumes looked right,

had sung Faust's famous aria "All hail, thou dwelling pure and lowly" with a good High C which was longly applauded, and I was, in general, quite proud of myself. But the Bible tells us what pride goeth before! For, in filling in with the agreed-upon acting, I suddenly felt my right gallus tear in two on the shoulder; but on the stage one does not adjust clothing, nor could I, since the broken suspender was far beneath my tight-fitting cavalier's costume and doublet. There was nothing to do but to hope and carry on. Mefisto drew me into the shade of the garden while Marguerite sang her "Ode to Night" from her balcony.

Trusting that the one remaining gallus would work for both, I followed our rehearsed acting scene, tore myself away from the Devil's power, bolted in long jumps across that wide, wide stage, leaped upon the flower-box under Marguerite's window and took the lovely lady into my arms. However, while doing all of this, the other suspender strap tore loose also and while we were there locked in each other's arms, my back to the audience, those free-wheeling tights nose-dived and dropped completely around my ankles! The audience roared. Moments later, holding the offending garments up as much as possible, I joined the others in curtain calls in trooper style. The audience called us back again and again.

Surely, never before had a Faust anywhere been more embarrassed or a Marguerite more flustered or an audience more amused. The local paper headlined the opera review with "FAUST TENOR LOSES PANTS ON STAGE."

Later on, through the kindness of a ballet-mistress who had seen what took place that night, I learned how to tie tights around one's middle with bias tape like professional dancers do to keep their tights from wrinking at the knees, and fortunately I never had "tights" troubles ever again.

Memories

*How memories crowd upon Time's tattered page
When we in recollection view the past!
We see our life laid bare without its age
And by no thoughts of idle fears harassed.
We see again the home where we were born
And all the childhood corners known so well;
These seem but weak reminders and forlorn
Of all that sings within our heart to tell.*

*Life's memories crowd. And through them once again
We live the days that now have passed away,
When we were wishing to be grown-up men
And do the things that then were only play.
But now as men, we view our childhood's yearn
With older heads and yet with hearts that burn.*

Catholics and Presbyterians

Italy is a Catholic country. I am a Presbyterian. The two beliefs have Christianity as a common meeting ground, of course, but my own belief, or so I have been taught to consider it, is the weaker of the two.

In the small rural community where I grew up in western Oklahoma, to be a Catholic was almost as incriminating as to be an infidel: you owed more loyalty to Rome than to God. Then, as a seventeen-year-old freshman at the University of Oklahoma, I was disappointed, even saddened, to learn that the Baptists had been outbid by the Catholics and had become the owners of a valuable building site on West Boyd Street in Norman for a girls' dormitory. As a backdrop perspective, these things were not conducive to attending Catholic mass in Italy when, following graduation, I went there for further study of music. It was hard to find a Protestant Church in Milan where I was studying; true, there was a small group of Swiss Protestants who held forth in an out-of-the-way address surrounded by whore-houses, and where one felt guilty of carnal sin even before entering the meeting room of the sect.

So it was that I swallowed my Presbyterian pride, prayed for forgiveness, and attended a Sunday morning mass in the great Milan Cathedral. Its architectural beauty is so enormous that one's mere churchly surroundings are a sermon fitting the needs of any soul and inspiring all sensitive persons to celestial glory. This taught me that the satisfaction of the Soul's Sincere Desire is more important than any other form of churchly communion, and that it is both the *Where* as well as the *What* that are important in one's personal worship. The vaulted heights of the Milan Cathedral and its flying expanses have many times lifted my earth-dirty soul into ecstatic dimensions of humble faith.

The second summer that I was in Europe, when the hot weather descended toward the end of June, I was flat broke. I didn't have the you-know-what to tangle with the cruel exchange on the Swiss franc which would have made possible the respite vacation in the coolness of the Swiss Alps that had been possible the preceding summer through careful early planning. There was little choice during this second summer, so I agreed to accompany the Lattuadas, the Milanese family with whom I lived, to Voghera, a community not far from Alessandria, where the famous Borsalino hats are manufactured. It was at Voghera where the Lattuadas' Aunt Petunia lived, and she would be expecting the big-city dwellers for their annual summer vacation at her house. Here they would continue to serve me, as the summer boarder, more of those cholesterol-filled but delicious meals that I enjoyed in Milan during the winter months of study. I took my final lesson of the spring term, thanked and kissed my beauteous teacher good-bye, and the Lattuadas and I left Milan the

CATHOLICS AND PRESBYTERIANS

next day on the "Slow Train Through Lombardy," traveling third class for so short a trip.

Soon after arriving at Aunt Petunia's in Voghera, I made the forced acquaintance of Giorgio, son of a neighbor, age seven years, and of his pet lamb, Fulcorina, age seven months. Like Mary's, whose fleece was white as snow, this ovine creature and her dirty whiteness were Giorgio's shadow. Giorgio's favorite uncle, the local priest, was stationed in Voghera, his home village, because his presence there solved some mental problems peculiar unto the man's rather far-out secular as well as sacred viewpoints. We became summertime friends. It was he who first told me about Don Lorenzo Perosi, composer extraordinary of Catholic sacred church music.

It was a pleasure to hear the local church choir which the priest directed. Even in rehearsals they were worth hearing, for what they lacked in quality they made up in quantity and in enthusiasm. Now, it must be remembered that Italians who speak well also sing well. This is because of the lack of constrictive sounds among their language's pure vowels. (How different that is from our own vocal mis-mash.) An interesting fact: some 90 per cent of all male voices in Italy are tenors. My teacher, Jean de Reszke, was once asked, in my presence, what countries produce, in his experience, the best of the high-and-low-keyed voices. He answered that his teaching experience had brought forth voices in quality as follows:

> Sopranos: United States and France
> Mezzos and Contraltos: England
> Tenors: Italy (without exception)
> Baritones and Basses: Russia, other Slavic countries

There are exceptions, of course, but the majority rules as written above.

Aunt Petunia had no piano, but I made arrangements with the local priest to use the upright piano in the church's choir rehearsal room for my own morning study. One day I found the priest already there and waiting to speak with me. He wanted to know if I had ever sung any of the Ave Marias in a Catholic church. By coincidence, I had with me in various albums or in sheet music the settings by Rosewig, Mascagni, Schubert, Cherubini, and Bach-Gounod, and I sang all of them for him that morning, playing my own accompaniments. He was generous in his praise and asked me to sing one of them the following Sunday at the eleven o'clock mass when the Bishop would be present. The priest chose the *Ave Maria* by Bach-Gounod since it was his own favorite and probably the best known of all the several musical settings of that ancient text. The church's organist was a young local butcher's apprentice who played the organ exceedingly well. We rehearsed at the seventeenth-century organ, and all was ready for a first-class rendition of this classic sacred song.

Sunday morning came, both of us had a bountiful breakfast, we warmed up, and when, in the mass our time came, we gave our best to the music. Then, Fulcorina, the she-lamb, appeared! Giorgio had taken the lamb early that morning, at his mother's order, to the other side of town and had tethered her on a slip-halter so that she could graze over a sizable space of grass, yet be confined to a certain area. The lamb evidently did not like the combination, or else she got lonesome by the time for the second mass. She had slipped her halter and was nearing Aunt Petunia's place as the final measures of the *Ave Maria* were being performed inside the church by the organist and me.

CATHOLICS AND PRESBYTERIANS

There are moments of psychological eloquence in our lives which sometimes speak more poignantly than any amount of words, be they human or animalistic, spoken or written. This unexpected arrival of Fulcorina at the church was one of those psychological moments. All had gone well with our treatment of the beautiful music and its Latin text, and as the final "Amen" was reduced to decrescendo like a heart-felt whisper, the organ and soloist seemed to unite into a single petition of praise to the Creator. Then WHAM! The voice of Fulcorina was heard in the land, not the voice of the Biblical turtle; and such a suddenly nasal and staccato percussiveness it had! The she-lamb walked down the aisle of the church as though she had been called to supper, bah-a--a-ing loudly with every step. Giorgio had been previously admonished by his mother to sit with the family; their pew included most of the entire next-to-the-front-center row. So, by the time that Giorgio had gotten out into the aisle and had led Fulcorina from the church, laughter reigned supreme among the congregation. Even the priest smiled broadly as he muttered something about even beasts praising their Creator.

Fulcorina's comment upon my singing was anything but sheepish, nor was it later surpassed by any human critic, either European or American. How many things there are to learn about animal nature as well as human nature. Many times since that day in Voghera I have sung the Bach-Gounod *Ave Maria*, even in churches of my own denomination for weddings or on concert programs, and each time, its sophisticated beauty always gives me a thrill; but the Voghera edition of the song's rendition was of a type completely peculiar unto itself. The echo of Fulcorina's nasal shimmy reduced me to proper size. She was truly my first helpful vocal critic.

Morning

At top of hill I stand
And watch the dawning of a new day.
At first, the chilly damp of night
Envelops all. And then, a ray

Of clear-cut light is thrown
Against the rosy canvas of the glowing east.
All Nature seems to feel the thrill
Of this new beacon of her coming priest.

New voices, wakened from the dew of quiet sleep,
Add their tumult to the rising chorus-cheer;
The sun, resolved anew to do his best,
Shines forth. And day is here.

The Darda Portrait

The portrait of me in colored chalk by Enrique Darda from Spain which is now hanging in the Oklahoma Hall of Fame's Museum, Oklahoma City, has an unusual story.

Generalissimo Franco of Spain took over the political control of his country during the 1930's and still holds sway there. Dissension against him was rampant wherever Spaniards gathered. And in New York where I was then living, it was especially marked. Wanting to raise money to help along the King of Spain and the Spanish Nationalists in their struggle against Dictator Franco, a group of world-famous Spanish musicians organized a Benefit Concert to be presented in Carnegie Hall. The list of performers included such luminaries as pianist José Iturbi, cellist Gaspar Cassado, and soprano Lucrezia Bori, to name but three. To add to the variety of the musical program, Miss Bori asked me to sing a pair of duets with her, one from Massenet's *Manon* which entire opera we had just been doing in performances at the Metropolitan Opera in New York, also one duet from Gounod's *Roméo et Juliette*.

In the New York *Times* I had been reading about the presence in New York then of Spain's noted portrait painter, Enrique Darda, and of how the socialites of Park Avenue were flocking to have him do their portraits. Imagine my surprise when Miss Bori telephoned to ask me to sit for my portrait, each performer's portrait to be reproduced in color on the brochure to be sold in the lobby of Carnegie Hall that evening, thus augmenting the Benefit's financial income. She asked that I telephone for an appointment and gave me the number. Mr. Darda did not speak English, Italian, or German but we got along well in French. He seized upon traits in only three sittings which a lens might have missed.

But the Benefit Concert was not given after all because it was prevented by our own United States government, which said that our nation could not take sides in someone else's civil war. Poor Mr. Darda found himself stuck with fourteen framed portraits, none of them ordered. I bought my own from him, but others did not. He doubtless has mixed emotions about the strange inhabitants of the United States.

Objects the size of this portrait are not permitted to be carried on New York subways, so I had to hire a taxi ($7.85, I remember) to get the picture to my apartment on West 57th Street. Weeks later my mother came to New York for a visit and, mother-like, discovered the portrait hiding in my closet. Nothing would do but to ship it to Norman, Oklahoma, to our home. To do this, I had to have a special shipping box made by a picture-framing shop which cost me another $25.00 and this, added to the Railway Express cost of transportation from New York to Norman, brought the total cost of the Darda portrait to a bit more than $200.00. After hanging on the walls of my home in Norman all of these years, the portrait has found its final niche. May it repose in peace!

Maestro Vittorio Maria Vanzo

Maestro Vittorio Maria Vanzo was a unique character and his personality as well as the instruction which he gave me influenced my life considerably. He had been a protégé of Queen Margherita of Italy who had paid out of her own personal funds for his instruction as a student of the piano at the Conservatorio in Milan, from which institution he had graduated with highest honors in his early twenties (in 1881).

The great German composer Richard Wagner fell ill, and in the autumn of 1882, having overextended his strength for the first performances of his opera *Parsifal* in Munich, decided that he could recoup his energies quicker and more pleasantly in Italy than elsewhere. So he leased the sizable house on Venice's Grand Canal which soon became known as the "Palazzo Wagner."

Among the letters of welcome from people of importance (some not even in Italy) was one from Queen Margherita, as citizen not as Queen; and in her letter she said that if Wagner needed anything which she as an Italian citizen, not as

Queen, could provide, please to say so. As was his wont, Wagner was quick to take her up on such an offer. He asked if she knew some really efficient and technique-wise pianist, a man who could read manuscripts as well as play the piano, who could come and live in the Palazzo Wagner in Venice and be on call to play the music which Wagner could write but not play. Naturally the Queen thought of Vanzo, her protégé, wrote to him in Milan, and Vanzo at once moved to the Palazzo Wagner in Venice and remained there at Wagner's beck and call until the great composer's death the following February.

Wagner was notably disordinate, his head being in the clouds most of the time in the manner of geniuses; and although he was a spendthrift with money and other things of value, he was curiously saving along certain unimportant lines. For example, he held on to old handwritten manuscripts even after the final edition had been published. Maestro Vanzo told me that oftentimes the only paper in the ornate marble bathroom of Palazzo Wagner would be pages from *Siegfried*, *Tristan und Isolde*, or Wagner's final opera, *Parsifal*; also, that on certain occasions Wagner would call Vanzo after midnight to come and play for him a new something which he had gotten out of bed himself to put on paper by the light of a single candle, his manuscript written like a cobweb, something to tax even young eyes. And should Vanzo hesitate in playing such feathery manuscripts, Wagner would go into a tantrum and in a mixture of German, Italian, and occasionally French, bawl out the young man for his having hesitated. And yet, Vanzo's affection for the great composer was genuine despite Wagner's occasional unreasonablenesses, a feeling which Vanzo admitted was a mixture of respect, affection, pity, and fear.

VITTORIO MARIA VANZO

Following Wagner's death of angina pectoris in his seventieth year, young Maestro Vanzo returned to Milan and soon advanced rapidly as an orchestra and opera conductor at the LaScala Opera House. It was he who first introduced Wagner's music to the Italian public; the work chosen as Wagner's first opera to be sung in Italy in Italian was *Siegfried*. The cast was contracted for eight performances that first season. The premiere was a sellout, Latin curiosity about a new work being then as today intense. Wagner's "far out" harmonies and constantly changing musical colors with unexpected dissonances almost caused a riot between opposite factions, with the result that at the second performance LaScala was almost empty. Maestro Vanzo persisted. Successive evenings produced similarly near-empty houses, but by the time the sixth performance came along, curiosity on the part of the public had returned and a sizable house came out. The seventh giving brought a full house; the eighth was the scene of standing-room-only; and to accommodate the demand for future tickets, three additional performances of *Siegfried* had to be given.

The following year other operas by Wagner were presented at LaScala and ever since then Wagner is one of the main spokes in the operatic wheel which causes LaScala to turn as the very hub of the world's opera. It was my good fortune during my student days in Milan to be able to attend the first complete giving of Wagner's *The Ring* at LaScala, directed by Arturo Toscanini. Nor shall I forget the edition of *Tristan und Isolde* which Toscanini prepared and directed, nor the opulent singing of the greatest singing-actress of that time, Giuseppini Cobelli (with whom later I was to sing eight performances of Cileà's opera *Adriana Lecouvreur*). According to Maestro Vanzo, *Tristan* was never a great success during his reign at LaScala, but he insisted that *Lohengrin* scored an instant success. Certain it is that today the Italian public holds both operas as dear possessions, especially *Lohengrin*.

In Norman there lived the family of the Victor Kulps. Dr. Kulp was Professor of Law at the University of Oklahoma and a native of the Chicago area. Mrs. Kulp was Swiss and when I went to study singing in Italy, she gave me a letter addressed to her mother, then a resident of Milan. Years before that, Mrs. Kulp (then Giuglia Koelliker) had had as seat-mate in the Swiss School in Via Principe Amadeo in Milan, a little girl named Amelita Galli who later on was to become Amelita Galli-Curci, the most famous coloratura soprano of her generation. Mrs. Kulp's mother, Frau Koelliker-Rothenbach, was a business woman dealing in international cotton and it was she who insisted that I study singing with Maestro Vanzo. It was Frau Koelliker who took me personally in a livery car to Maestro Vanzo's studio after making an audition appointment over the telephone.

Maestro Vanzo was in his early seventies when we first met and I studied with him almost daily for about two years, returning for occasional lessons later between opera seasons in various parts of Europe. After our last lesson of coaching on Puccini's *Madama Butterfly* Maestro Vanzo presented to me, as a gift, three pages of music printed in Japan from which Puccini had taken some authentic Oriental melodies used in the first act of the opera and with first-edition notations in pencil in Puccini's own handwriting along the margins. In 1944 I gave this music to the Music Library of the University of Oklahoma along with Maestro Vanzo's copy of Wagner's life story entitled *Ma Vie* which Maestro Vanzo wanted me to have. The gift also included some letters of Giuseppe

Verdi, and Richard Strauss written in their own handwriting.

Maestro Vanzo was an inspirational teacher whose outspoken, gruff manner had to be understood but who, because of such manner, enabled his pupils to receive vocal and operatic verism without camouflage or in half-truths. All tenor roles in the Wagner operas are for dramatic voices. I only regret that my smaller lyric sound was not capable of having received the instruction and the great traditions for Wagnerian roles which Maestro Vanzo above all others then living could have given me; yet from him I gained many timeless truths of operatic singing and other traditions, and shall ever be grateful to him for his patience with my ignorance and for the inspiration of his own abrasive personality with which he tried to file off some of my own rough spots both as a person and as a young singer.

Evening

Wondrous hues upon the western sky,
The sigh of cattle upon a grassy slope;
Fresh fragrance borne from new-cut hay:
And evening comes.

The colors sink below the western rim;
On high a star sends forth its wavering beam;
A quiet hush descends on all the land:
And day is gone.

Regarding Ernestine Schumann-Heink

The first time that I ever heard the great German contralto Ernestine Schumann-Heink sing was in recital at the no-longer-existing Overholser Theatre (called "The Opera House" in those days) in Oklahoma City. This was in the Spring of 1917. Because of a mix-up in tickets mailed too late to arrive on time (perhaps on purpose, as we found out later from others who complained), my host, William G. Schmidt, my voice teacher at the University of Oklahoma, and I were seated instead on the front row on the stage quite near the piano.

As style authorities know, no woman who is short and heavy set should ever wear lustrous satin or light colors, both of which exaggerate the wearer's size; and most of all, never a train on a formal gown unless the wearer is correspondingly tall. Madame Schumann-Heink that evening wore all three no-nos of formal sophistication: a gown of yellow slipper satin with fishtail train. At her appearance on the stage, which was crowded with the overflow of patrons seated in folding-chairs, there was cordial applause. She bowed her thanks and proceeded to the curve of the grand piano. But one of the steel tacks holding in place the white canvas floor covering where she would walk near the piano caught, and before she could realize what was taking place, had torn off about two feet of the train's trailing length!

Her lady accompanist picked up the torn-off piece and was starting to take it backstage when Schumann-Heink with girlish exaggeration took the piece of cloth out of the accompanist's hands, walked to the piano and dropped the cloth on the top of the instrument, saying in a loud voice: "Vell! unt vhat doo you teenk off dott!" This gesture of unabashed *Gemütlichkeit* so endeared her to the audience that she would not have had to sing at all to have won over her auditors. When she returned for the program's second group of songs, we noticed that her lady accompanist had pinned the torn part so that the skirt length was about the same all of the way around. Some twenty years later in Chicago, I told Madame Schumann-Heink that I was in the audience that evening. She remembered the incident distinctly.

During the season of 1934-35, Madame Schumann-Heink had a series of radio broadcasts which emanated from Chicago and which advertised a brand of baby foods. One of her good friends in Chicago was my father's cousin who only a short time before that had lost her only brother. I was then in my first season with the Chicago Opera, and for the sake of companionship it was my cousin's wish that I make her house my headquarters. Madame Schumann-Heink was then living at the Park Lane Hotel on North Michigan Avenue where we visited her and enjoyed some of the fine German food she loved to prepare. She bought all ingredients a block west on Clark Street "because groceries are cheaper there."

ERNESTINE SCHUMANN-HEINK

On the late afternoons of her radio-broadcast days, it was the pleasant routine for my cousin and me to take a taxi from the cousin's home at 2450 Lake View Avenue, stop by the Park Lane Hotel and get the good lady (she would be waiting punctually just inside the main entrance door, never did we once have to wait for her), then proceed to the Mercantile Mart to the radio studio, hear her do the orchestra rehearsal, then broadcast, have a hot soup with her, then reverse the trip by taxi northward. On one of these evenings, as we were on our way in a cab, the good lady said that she had sung badly at times during that evening's broadcast. "I vass skairt," she confessed. From one of the pull-up seats in the taxi, I inquired if she still was frightened after her many years before the public. "Yah, yah, unt yah. You singh best venn you skairt!" How very right she was.

The Quiet Sea

*The sea is smooth and calm today
As shimmering ripples dance and play
Across each wave that is a part
Of the mighty ocean's twilight heart.*

*But here above that cold and night
Where not even fishes are given sight,
The ripples run and romp away
Like happy children on a holiday.*

*But storms will come upon the sea
And waves will dash in wild fury,
And no resemblance will there be
Of today's tranquility.*

Amelita Galli-Curci

The first time that I ever heard Amelita Galli-Curci was in Oklahoma City. Two years previous she had made her American debut with the Chicago Opera as Gilda in *Rigoletto* and had literally stopped the show. In Oklahoma City she sang in recital at the Livestock Barn of the State Fair Grounds when they were at the extreme east end of East Fourth Street, at the end of the East Fourth streetcar line. I had no money to buy a ticket so I ushered to get to hear the great lady, going up from Norman on the 1:07 P.M. Santa Fe, returning that same night on the 1:35 A.M. caboose. It made for a long day.

Mr. Hathaway Harper was the concert manager who brought the new singer to Oklahoma. We ushers had to report at the Livestock Barn at 7:00 P.M. for instructions. In going out on the East Fourth streetcar it so happened that my seat was just behind the diva's flutist; their manager was seated next to him, and for the first time in my whole life I was hearing Italian spoken. I was enchanted! As I had done when ushering to hear the performance of the Chicago Opera the preceeding spring, as soon as possible, without being too obvious, a folding chair was hidden by me in the men's room and later retrieved and placed in the exact middle of the front row of the $7.00 seats where I heard the rest of the evening's music in the style of a grand pasha.

I have already referred to Dr. Victor Kulp, noted world-authority on Petroleum Law at the University of Oklahoma, and Mrs. Kulp, who had been a schoolmate of Amelita Galli (Galli-Curci) in Milan. Little did I dream, on that evening, that the course of my own life was later to be altered by Mrs. Kulp's mother, the same Signora Koelliker who "discovered" Amelita Galli-Curci. This Amelita Galli was a promising pianist and had been the piano teacher of Mrs. Victor Kulp's sister, Elsa Koelliker. Later she was to develop the stupendous vocal technique which carried her to international acclaim as one of the greatest coloratura sopranos of all time. Her voice was discovered as follows:

It was then, and still is today, the custom in Italy for piano lessons to be given in the home of each pupil. Signorina Galli's mother was dead, and the daughter and her father, who was in poor health, lived in a small flat in the Porto Nuovo section of Milan. The daughter earned a modest living for both of them by giving piano lessons in the homes of pupils. This special lesson-day Elsa Koelliker was having difficulties with a certain passage in the piano composition being studied. Its fingering seemed so awkward and after several unsuccesses as to what to do with it and its wrong notes, the teacher demonstrated the notes of the difficult passage with her voice. At that moment, the pupil's mother was passing through the adjoining room and heard what the teacher had done vocally. "Amelita, was that you?" she asked. "Yes, Signora, I'm trying to help Elsa get these notes right."

AMELITA GALLI-CURCI

"Do that again with your voice, please," said the older woman, and the young teacher complied. That day's discovery that the little piano teacher from Porto Nuovo could sing so exquisitely was the beginning of an illustrious career. As she was later to do with me, Signora Koelliker took the young woman to Vittorio Vanzo, the Italian protégé of Richard Wagner, then first-conductor at the LaScala Opera House who coached her for several months, later making it possible for her to get needed operatic experience with small traveling companies. It was during one of the tours with a small company in Sicily that a conductor from the Chicago Opera heard her and opened up negotiations with the management which resulted in her being engaged by the Chicago Opera. It was also during these barnstorming tours of Southern Italy that Amelita Galli had met young Luigi Curci, and they had been married. So it was that she adopted both her own and her husband's names and came to the United States as Amelita Galli-Curci.

As soon as the recital program was over in Oklahoma City, I rushed backstage along with others to see the diva and perhaps to get her autograph; but the door to her improvised dressing room was barred by a burly policeman who shooed all of us youngsters away with unmistakable gestures. After several minutes the door opened and out came both the diva and Mrs. Kulp, their arms around each other. They walked through the crowd, got into a car and drove away. I was quite impressed.

Years later, after graduation with two degrees from the University of Oklahoma, subsequent study of voice in Chicago, followed by twenty-two months as a pupil of Jean de Reszke in France, I was spending the summer at home getting reacquainted with my parents. One day Mrs. Kulp telephoned my mother to say that she had read in the Norman *Transcript* that I was soon to go for further vocal study to Milan, Italy and wondered if I would be kind enough to take her step-mother in that city a gift which Mrs. Kulp had made by hand. Of course, my mother said that I would be pleased to take the gift. When the Kulp son, Albert, then a student in Norman High School, brought it to our home, it proved to be a sizable bundle, a hand-made quilt for a single bed. My cabin-size trunk was already packed for my departure and it was bursting-full. What to do? The problem was solved by my mother (as is so often so with mothers). She took my winter overcoat off its hanger in the trunk and put the folded quilt in its place, saying that my overcoat had already seen eight years of service and that I was to leave it at home for the Salvation Army and could buy a new coat when the weather in Italy got cold. This was done.

No one had told me who Mrs. Kulp's mother was; I had only her name and address in Milan. That cabin-trunk got held up at Cherbourg and did not arrive in Milan until two weeks after I did but the day that I took the quilt to Signora Koelliker happened to be her birthday. Not knowing Italian, the first few weeks in Milan I spoke French when I had to speak at all, French being a required subject in all of the schools of northern Italy. And, in turn, the Milanese pronounced my family name with the slant which only the French language can give it. At my small hotel in Via Larga, Milan, I had asked how to get to the address of Signora Koelliker and was told to take such-and-such a streetcar, change twice, and that the address was some seven kilometers distant.

When I got there, I found the address to be in a manufacturing part of the city, the precise number to be the headquarters of the world's next-to-largest cotton wholesalers, and that Signora Koelliker was the president of the entire company. To get in to see her I had to pass through the offices (and hands) of two separate secretaries, to each of whom I had to explain in French and an occasional word of Italian who I was and what was wanted. But the fact that it was on her birthday that the gift was being delivered and that it had been handmade by her stepdaughter in far-off America melted the crusty exterior of the president of the company (Clark's Thread), and she gave me a warm welcome. A few evenings later, she invited me to dinner in the family's home upstairs over the offices, the first in a long series of such associations with her and her large family, which are among the most pleasant memories of my eleven and one-half years of residence and of singing in European opera houses. The same Beckstein piano was still there at which Amelita Galli had sung the notes with which her young piano pupil had had difficulty, and I used to play upon it when no one was there. It served for accompaniment also when Signora Koelliker would have me sing during the musicales she gave twice yearly in her beautiful home.

In the town of Saronno, north of Milan, the Koelliker family owned a summer place. The grounds were extensive, the orchard well attended, the vegetable garden productive, and in the villa itself were some valuable items of medieval art. On the second floor of the villa was the long living room with original sixteenth-century frescoes on its ceiling and handsome colored mural painting on its walls, all of them soft and mellow but still glowing with vibrant colors. The Bechstein concert piano was in that room, its image reflected in the polished mosaic-wood floor, and from the villa's north and west casement windows there was a stunning view of the

Alps. In fact, from the position of the bed in the room I used to occupy on week-ends, I could lie abed and watch the dawn illuminating first the very top of Monte Rosa, then creeping down its icy slopes until the entire forest-covered sides and the intervening valleys were in rosy light. It was difficult on such Monday mornings to get out of bed and prepare to return to the heat and humidity of Milan and resume the grind of studying how to holler.

Ostend and the Locked-in Keys

Following the opera season during July and August of 1929 in the Arena of Verona, Italy, where that summer's production of Mascagni's opera *Isabeau* and of Gounod's *Faust* had been among the most successful ever presented in that venerable ancient Roman amphitheatre, in order to make rail connections on first-class trains up north, I had to leave Verona on the night train for Ostend, Belgium. The management of the Verona Arena, ex-notable tenor Giovanni Zenatello and famous-for-her-Carmen mezzo Maria Gay had booked me with Sayag and Associates as soloist with the Symphonie Royale Belge in Ostend for two concerts in two days, and almost without time for rehearsals with the orchestra. (The end of August is always the "Haute Saison" in Ostend.)

In Milan, in those days, there lived an American lady friend of our family's—a lady whose dress size was precisely that of my mother's; they could easily wear each others' dresses. Those were the beginning days of satin-backed crepe, out of proportion to pay for when findable and complicatedly difficult to find in shops or stores. This American friend had a Milanese ladies' tailor whose talents were truly remarkable and who later on, so I was told, became the star cutter in the home shop in Paris of the designer, Jean Patou. It had been four years since I had been home. I wanted to bring my parents as gifts some of the beautiful but also useful things of Italy. It was decided that, for my mother, her gift would be a three-piece suit of midnight blue satin-backed crepe (if findable) and tailored with the good taste of the ladies' tailor. So it was that we had the American family friend be the model for my mother's dress and by so doing were sure that the dress would fit when I brought it to her on my visit home. For my father, I had my own tailor make him a handsome gray-and-red woolen house-jacket.

Since I would be sailing from the northern part of Europe, it suddenly occurred to me that it would become mandatory to pay customs charges on the contents of my trunk at the frontiers of Austria, Switzerland, Germany, Holland, and Belgium as well as when arriving in New York, and that such would be like rebuying these items several times over. I appealed to the Milan branch of the American Express Company, and they said that the trunk could be sent "in bond," that is, sealed until arrival at the port of destination, which in this case would be New York; thus only one import tax would have to be paid, not six. I delivered the stateroom-sized Hartman trunk containing the dress and some of my better suits to the "in bond" clerk and put into my billfold the typed instructions which the clerk gave me about opening the trunk at Ostend for examination by Belgian customs authorities before the German Line transported it across the Atlantic, this, to see if by chance it had been tampered with en route from Italy. All moved smoothly until after the time for opening the trunk for customs examination at Ostend.

I was scheduled to sail on the *SS Deutschland* of the German Line from Belgium to New York, the ship's departure being on Sunday at 1:00 P.M. My two appearances as soloist with the Symphonie Royale Belge were on Friday night and Saturday in matinee. Every free moment was spent rehearsing with the orchestra the various arias I was to sing, so it was not possible to visit the customs office until Sunday morning. Now, the Ostend customs office on Sunday mornings does not open until 10:00 A.M. I did not know this until getting there much earlier than that. The customs officer assigned me by the main office was an unpleasant person with a cow-like face and the tic of a twitching nose like that of the Belgian hares he later on mentioned raising. All was in order with the trunk sent "in bond" from Milan. I opened the trunk, showed its contents, signed all necessary papers and was preparing to close an inside drawer when without cause or reason the customs officer slammed the lid of my trunk. It locked and my keys were on the inside!

All along it had been difficult to communicate with this customs inspector since he, like most of the people of Ostend, spoke only Flemish. (Flemish is a mixture of Low German, gutteral Holland Dutch, and a dirty brand of scabby French.) These custom inspectors would look cow-like at you whenever you addressed them in French, High German, or English and, of course, were utterly mute when spoken to in Italian. What to do?

The man who had brought me all of this anxious woe took it as a daily occurrence (and perhaps it was for him). He had nothing to suggest except to show me the address of a locksmith who just "might" be able to undo on Sunday the wrong which this customs officer had done. In short, I hired a taxi by the hour and went to four different addresses in as many parts of the city before finding someone who could open the slammed-shut trunk. It being Sunday, I had visions of a price in blood for the service sought, but was pleasantly surprised when the bill amounted to only about $12.00 in American money plus three hours of taxi-fare. I was near-frantic several times, though, during the ticklish procedure when I saw how fast the clock's hands were turning and how slowly and without success those lumbering locksmiths were stalling.

The *SS Deutschland* sailed at 1:00 P.M. I boarded the tender taking passengers out to the big ship stationed in deep water only minutes before the ship boomed her throaty whistle. I was both glad and thankful that my first experience with "in bond" shipments had turned out even as well as it had, but never again have I used such service. Slammed trunk lids cause too much worry to ugly Americans. Besides, if used again anywhere in the world, I might be assigned that same kook.

Our Opera Season in Tripoli

In 1928, Libya, North Africa, was a colony of Italy. Mussolini had plans and hopes of making Tripoli to Italy what Sicily had been to Greece in ancient times: the part of the dominion which supplied most of the fruit, grain, wool, clothing, leather, and politicians for the entire realm. The business economy of North Africa in 1928 was flourishing and the city of Tripoli, capital of the enormous desert province of Libya, was fast becoming the center of provincial Italian culture of the local Fascist brand, filled with secret meetings and unresolved vendettas.

All of the Italian press of that period was completely under the political thumb of the Fascist Party, and readers (if we read the front page at all) were regaled by headlines and flashy articles of doubtful journalism extolling the glowing wonders of the desert country's manner of being governed which made all of this possible. We also had to listen to political singing in chorus *ad nauseum* about how right Italian citizens were to move their residence to one of the new settlements along the shores of North Africa, no matter how deep went the roots of their families into the maternal soil of Italy during past centuries. It was somewhat like a political carnival or perhaps a continuous Saturday afternoon circus.

So it was that when Manlio Pasotto, the Milan impresario who had made possible my opera debut in Italy, asked if I would be interested in being one of the three tenors in the company he was organizing to play for two months in a new opera house in Tripoli, at once I said yes. I was to receive a small salary (small since I was a raw recruit and had never done any of the operas to be assigned me), but gratis would be my round-trip transportation by sea, Genoa–Tripoli, together with all meals aboard the ship and a private stateroom.

Italian impresarios as a rule are looking out for Number One (themselves) and are noted for trying in clever and conniving ways to fleece financially gullible Americans anxious to make an Italian opera debut. A part of human psychology is that desire to flaunt something in selfish ecstasy over the heads of one's peers. Such sort of agreement with a dishonest impresario would give forth perhaps a printed program to take home, also occasionally a brief "review" (really a newsitem) in the provincial press. (We Americans will believe anything if it comes to us in print.) But I found Manlio Pasotto to be honest and usually ready to "play ball" as regards a financial understanding. Being a disappointed tenor himself, he demanded and got the best singing from his cast which each member could give. From him I learned much about the lyric theatre, how it is run, also some things regarding what a manager has to do to organize, present, and clean up the artistic litter after a season of opera, be such in the metropolitan cities or in some obscure provincial opera house.

IN TRIPOLI

Knowing this man helped my understanding of opera and caused new respect for those hard-working men and women who make opera seasons possible.

The opera season in Tripoli was to include twenty-four performances of six different operas and three of that number were to be operas I was prepared to sing (for the first time, of course). The day after arriving by sea, we began rehearsals in a flat-floored warehouse where the echo was annoying; and since it was next door to the new opera house the noise of stone-masons and the whining of electric saws drilled into our ears. Even in those days, labor unions had strikes. There was a strike among plasterers going on when we arrived and it naturally slowed the finishing of the new theatre. Since every day meant money, three groups of scab workmen, each group with two headmen, were put upon the job. They worked around-the-clock, the night shift working under enormous blue arc-lights. In about eight days the work was done enough so that we could rehearse on the new stage. We felt as if Santa Claus had arrived.

One of the attractive sights of the new opera house was the impromptu electric fixtures hanging from the high ceilings both in the theatre and in the foyer. The supply house in Naples which was to have furnished the crystal-and-steel lighting fixtures failed to get them there on time. The Arab women then stepped in and literally made their own brand of lighting fixtures. They took old discarded iron wheels, soldered two of them together at right angles for each fixture, then covered all spaces in between the spokes with local linen cloth dyed an intense indigo blue. The light of the electric bulbs shining through those thicknesses of blue cloth cast a blue light of ethereal beauty over everything beneath them; even after the ordered fixtures arrived, the blue linen-covered ones were kept. As lighting fixtures go, nothing could be more of a conversation-piece or novel.

By means of the grapevine, as well as an occasional hint in the local newspaper, it was noised about that the King of Italy was coming to Tripoli to inaugurate the Spring Fair, a commercial undertaking amounting to a large sum of money to the tradespeople of the colony. It was announced also that all tourist trips to Leptis Magna and other ancient Roman ruins many miles across the desert would be discontinued after a certain date, then resumed following the King's return to Rome. I hurried to buy a ticket and took this interesting trip, daily rehearsals permitting. (What a smart bunch of engineers those ancient Romans were! They built for coming centuries.)

The King of Italy came and great was the noise of his coming. Every store put on its best facade and washed its windows; that, in a land where water is so scarce, *is an achievement*. And what was most thrilling to us of the opera house was that their Majesties came for the last two acts of the opera the evening of their arrival (a complete surprise even to the management). The opera was *Rigoletto*. Royal police literally took over the opera house for security reasons, and so nervously excited was the soprano that, when in the acting I touched her hand, it was like ice. Well, after all, not every Italian soprano in those days of the Italian Monarchy could sing "Gilda" before the Sovereigns of her land—at least, not too frequently.

We had opened the season in Tripoli with *Madama Butterfly* and it was emotionally moving to observe how hungry local Italian settlers were for the beautiful melodies of Puccini. Some of the audience were so moved that they wept at hearing them. A feature article in *La Gazetta* had said that I was American. After one of the *Madama Butterfly* performances, a dear old lady came up to me and said, "Signore, your being an American, you should know. Tell me: are all American men fickle and mean like the American in *il Maestro's* opera?" What could one answer? I tried to explain to her that there are all kinds of men in all countries and that among American men there are men good and true as well as fickle like Pinkerton in *Madama Butterfly*. She seemed little convinced and kept mumbling and gesticulating as she left.

It was illuminating to note how Italians "make do" when they have so little to work with. An example: because of popular demand, many more performances of *Madama Butterfly* were given than were originally scheduled, the result being that the soprano doing the title role used up all of the eye shadow which is so needed when an Occidental plays an Oriental. It was impossible to buy make-up in Tripoli then, so the soprano burned the lower part of a cork, mixed the ash with vaseline and face cream and thus did not have to be embarrassed by borrowing from a rival soprano.

There are a few oases deep in the southern part of Libya, most of which were in the hands of Bedouins. Most other parts of the arid waste were hostile to man, and yet, certain ones had enough dates and even olives to warrant the cost of transporting them by camel to the North Shore Country and the city of Tripoli. I well remember the trains of loaded camels, heavy with dates or olives, padding patiently down the street in front of my rented room on their way to the public market. This to the eye was surely the Orient, yet it spoke Italian.

It is always difficult to get to do a new opera for the first time. In Tripoli I did seven performances of three operas and each for the first time. They were *Madama Butterfly*, *La*

Bohème, and *Rigoletto*. Each one meant money in my pocket when looking toward the future.

The opera-thirsty public had been filling the new opera house nightly so the season was extended evening by evening or until the "Ghiblee" might start. The Ghiblee is a cruel wind blowing from the desert. It begins when the cold of the water of the Mediterranean Sea pulls the hot wind of the Sahara unto itself and brings the dreadful dust storms feared by all. It is impossible to put a calendar date on the arrival of the Ghiblee since the heat of the desert is variable; but come it will, every year toward the end of May.

As it turned out, the final evening's offering was again the ever-popular *Rigoletto*. All had gone normally during Acts I and II, but as I was singing *"Parmi veder le lagrime"* which opens Act III, all at once there was an ominous noise like gas escaping, and before I knew for sure what was happening, all that I could see of the conductor was his white shirt front. The Ghiblee had arrived! And with it tons of dust from the desert. It was impossible to sing; nor could the music be heard because of the general coughing. The remainder of the performance was canceled, and the audience and we got home as soon and as best we could. I gathered my LaScala-made *Rigoletto* costumes together, put them in a large theatrical suitcase, and pulling against that heavy wind, walked back to my rented room, where it was easy to see how much dust had settled already by the visible coating atop my bedspread. It took me the remainder of the night to pack my other belongings. At 8:00 A.M. we sailed on the *SS Sardinia* for Naples and Genoa. It was fine to have a bath aboard the ship! The salary I had earned during those two months had paid for my board and room; I had learned a lot, had put three operas into repertory, and was on the road to operatic success! Hooray for Tripoli!

The Oratorio "Moses" at Treviso

The unwanted bleating of Fulcorina, the she-lamb belonging to young Giorgio at Voghera and the disturbance she caused in the local church service where I had sung Bach-Gounod's *Ave Maria*, took place in July of 1926. The bishop of the diocese had promised to be present that morning but had been prevented from coming by the failure of his car to start, and it being Sunday, he could find no one to repair the balky motor. In his stead it so happened that there came a far more important personage to me, Don Licinio Refice, whose assigned work was director of the choir of Rome's church of Santa Maria Maggiore; but it was summertime and Don Licinio was on vacation.

An introverted priest, he overstepped his usual lack of sociability and came back to the choir room following the mass in order to speak with me. He said that he had written several oratorios himself, and that the new oratorio *Moses* written by his colleague Don Lorenzo Perosi had been accepted as one of the featured works during the short opera season of the coming May in the city of Treviso, north of Venice on the road to Vienna. Would I be interested in auditioning for the solos allotted to the tenor? I would. We exchanged written postal addresses but I did not hear from him further until three years later when my agent called to ask if I might possibly be interested in having him sign me for an undetermined number of performances of an oratorio written by a priest. The oratorio was to be given a featured place during the opera season that May in Treviso. The town's chorus was noted for walking away yearly with prizes in competition throughout all of northern Italy. My agent said that the oratorios title was *Moses* and that it was written by a priest named Don Lorenzo Perosi. My agent was against my signing for any sort of oratorio performances, but I insisted that it would be a novel experience and also a fresh break from opera, opera, opera.

The annual season of summer performances in the Arena of Verona was of such importance that the oratorio performances at Treviso, which came so near to the Verona season, were almost obliterated by the bigger international events. I had studied my solos well and was ready for the public presentation of the churchly, harmonically satisfying music and the even beauty of the wedding between the Latin text and the rhythmic charms of the choral passages. The local orchestra was highlighted by key instrumental soloists brought in from Venice, Graz, and Vienna. The oratorio was presented in the fifteenth-century Duomo or Cathedral of Treviso which has pictures on its walls painted by Titian. Treviso is the ancient "Tarvisium" of Roman centuries, and it was also distinguished for being a member of the ancient Lombard League. Today it is a forward-looking city of some 50,000 persons.

AT TREVISO

The Latin text of the oratorio tells of the trials of Moses as a leader of the Hebrew people. The protagonist's music is assigned to the baritone voice, but the most important part musically is given over to the mixed chorus and is done in masterful writing. This shows with what love Don Lorenzo wrote for his beloved choirs; after all, it was his life work. We gave four performances of this oratorio in Treviso, each one attended by a capacity audience and lasting three full hours. So great was the demand for tickets after the success of the opening evening that we added an extra performance which caused me to be up all night in order to get to the Arena in Verona for rehearsals of *Faust* which I was to do in the scheduled summer opera program. How tired can one get!

Don Licinio Refice had heard the final two performances of *Moses* in Treviso. He now set about casting the opera *Cecilia* which he had written, and hoped to have produced in the Royal Opera House in Rome. He could do so provided he could get the written consent and blessing of the Pope; the question of Church and State, even under Fascist rule, was ever present. Don Licinio Refice's semi-sacred opera *Cecilia*, being an opera written by a priest, who was trying to get it produced by the State (Royal) Opera House, brought forth a shower of fresh politics. The Royal Opera of Rome was lukewarm to the proposition, the Vatican even less warm.

But Don Licinio Refice was a good politician and the lobbying which he and his friends displayed worked wonders. He had taught a course at the Pontifical High School in Rome called "Sacred Music" for many, many years, so he had a few loyal graduates to help him in his campaign for getting his opera produced by the State Opera. It was this same kindly aggressiveness which enabled the good man to direct, inspire, and manage the 1947 tour of ninety-nine concerts of "The Roman Singers of Sacred Music" throughout the United States. It was an enormous success; only the American tours of the Sistine Choir had more spectacuular acclaim.

We shall be hearing of Don Licinio Refice again and soon.

The Arena of Verona

As the popes in Rome gained in temporal power during the early centuries, so grew also the difficulties of communication and transportation between the North and the South zones of the Papacy, and it became apparent that there was crying need for an "Assistant Pope" somewhere between Rome and the Alps. In those days it was a week's journey each way overland between the North and Rome. So it was decided to make Verona the seat of an Assistant or Second Popedom.

To keep human rabble satisfied, two things are needed: (1) bread and (2) sports. To fill the need for sports, the Arena was built in Verona. Only somewhat smaller than the Coliseum in Rome, the Arena of Verona saw some of the bloodiest battles ever known to man. In fact, the word "arena" means sand. It was sand that absorbed the puddles of blood and allowed the ghoulish games to proceed during the big days of visiting celebrities. The "Second Vatican" in Verona lasted for several centuries or until invasions from the North caused the powers of this second-rate Papacy to wane.

Although the Arena remains today magnificent, it is evident that it too has had to withstand its enemies. It seems that the city of Verona lies atop an earthquake fault. Tragically, the Arena lost many of its terraced seats during past centuries, including the top-most tier of stone benches. From the rubble, already-cut stones have been stolen for use as stones for new houses of various generations. Today there are forty-three tiers of limestone steps which give access to the interior of the Arena; these have been repaired and rebuilt piecemeal ever since the earthquakes of the sixteenth century. Today, in the summer, the Arena is used for evening performances of opera. These audiences are so critical about singing that they are only somewhat less bloodthirsty than the throngs of centuries past who came to see gladiators and other strongmen kill each other.

The natives of that part of Italy have long been noted for their blood-letting criticism of opera singing, and numerous are the debutants whose bubble of success has popped either at Verona's wintertime season in the downtown Opera House or the summertime season in the Arena. If an opera debutant satisfies the public of Verona, Parma, and the people living near Bologna, he can face without fear almost any other opera audience in the world.

The Cathedral of Verona is a handsome church, a real attraction of the city. Its construction was finished, records show, in 1187. Its graceful altar is by Titian. Verona was the original home-base residence of the Scala family whose encouragement of opera in Italy is legendary. Too, the town's women have long been noted for their beauty and grace; writers from Shakespeare in his time to André Malraux in today's attest to such fact (and was not Juliette a Veronese beauty?).

THE ARENA OF VERONA

One of the very few bridges built by the Romans and still in use anywhere stands in Verona and spans the swift Adige River. It is built of limestone and appears to date from not too long after Christ. A modern bridge of steel and concrete was built during the 1920's by Fascist command and located near the old Roman bridge, to divert some of the international motor traffic away from its venerable neighbor, and also to prove to doubters that the Fascist régime could justly vaunt itself in the difficult art of bridge building. But during the time that I was singing at the Arena in July and August of 1929, the supposedly unsurpassed techniques of those Fascist engineers came to nothingness, for the late thaw in the Alps joined with heavy rains in the hill country to the north and o-u-t went the modern mistake of steel and cement, in spite of its builders' bragging. All local as well as international motor traffic had to be shunted over the faithful stone arches of the Roman bridge, which for so many centuries have carried man in his desire or need to get to the other side of the river.

Some of my enlarged snapshots show the flood waters of the Adige River rushing under these ancient, eroded blocks of Roman limestone, some of which are as large and as gnarled as the stones in the Egyptian Pyramids.

It was during this 1929 summer opera in Verona that I first met Miss Eva Turner, the noted British dramatic soprano, today "Dame" Eva. We were members of the same opera company in Verona that summer but were never cast in the same performance. She was singing *Isabeau* by Mascagni and I was doing Gounod's *Faust*. Whenever Miss Turner had sung at LaScala, in Milan, I had noticed that the prices were higher than regularly. She commanded universal respect both personally and professionally and was regarded by everyone to be the greatest Turandot of all time. My Italian landlady in Milan compared every soprano she heard on record or on the air with the brilliant singing of the lass from Lancashire whom the good signora called "Mees Toorn-air."

Now, Mascagni's *Isabeau* is rarely given in any country, so every member of the stage group and of the cast had to learn his or her part in the score from scratch. The public responded to the first performance chiefly out of curiosity. Since the staging was lavish and the sets and costumes necessarily showy for such vast surroundings, it was instantly noised about that *Isabeau* was worth seeing as well as hearing. Alternating with *Isabeau* starring Eva Turner, Hippolito Lazzaro, and Salvatore Baccaloni, was Gounod's *Faust* with Gina Cigna, Ezio Pinza, and me. The weather was perfect for outdoor opera and spending an evening with fine music is something to remember always.

To give some basis of comparison as to the relative size of the stage of LaScala and of the Arena of Verona, let me say that at LaScala, in Franchetti's opera *Germania*, I saw six loads of hay pulled by twelve draft horses abreast move from back-stage toward the audience without the stage's seeming crowded; also that in *Aida* at LaScala, some 350 persons in the Triumphal Scene marched and gesticulated in operatic fashion but never bumped into or collided with their neighbors.

The stage of the Verona arena, however, is so vast that to get to a required spot in time, we had to start from the wings or wherever far earlier than on a normal-sized stage. Let me add, too, that the sight of those acres of human beings (26,000 on opening night of our *Faust*) was enough to frighten one into complete vocal silence. This was, of course, before the days of microphones on the stage; it was a question of reaching your public personally or going home tomorrow.

Since there was no upper proscenium from which curtains could be suspended, dazzle-lights were mounted on small elevators (lifts) hidden in the floor and controlled by a master switch causing them to rise to the height of a man standing and shine into the eyes of the audience during intermissions or other times when scenery was being moved into position for the following act.

The dressing rooms of the soloists at the Verona Arena were originally the cages and dens of wild animals brought to the amphitheatre to fight with professional gladiators or with other wild animals. A semblance of modernity had been installed to make us more comfortable, but when compared with the usual theatrical accommodations, those at Verona's Arena were quite on the "make-do" variety.

The story of *Isabeau* resembles that of Lady Godiva, which means that in the final scene the soprano, completely nude, must mount a white charger and ride rapidly from the stage. The way that Miss Turner managed this strip-tease without letting it be cheap or objectionable was remarkable. Yes, Italians are hot-blooded, but they resent obscenity on the stage, and they loved the way in which Miss Turner handled this thistle-sharp circumstance: she wore an all-over set of skin-tights and a blonde wig of below-the-waist length which had been made precisely for her by wig-maker Biffi of La-Scala. These items combined to make the scene spicy but also critic-proof. Musically, *Isabeau* at times reminds one of the same composer's *Cavalleria Rusticana*.

The *Isabeau* score is orchestrated with a heavy hand, and since the music is most generally loud and a bit gaudy with each end-of-act in rising volume proportions, the Latins loved it. No paid advertising was needed. After the opening night, publicity by word-of-mouth sold all of the seats in that huge amphitheatre. This was true with *Faust* as well as with *Isabeau*.

On opening night *Faust* drew a total of 26,000 listeners inside the Arena and several hundred more outside who could not even buy standing-room. Those loyal opera followers that evening literally shouted their joy at Papa Gounod's lovely tunes and declaimed without a shadow of doubt the High C in the tenor's "*Salve, dimora casta e pura.*"

My Marguerite in those *Faust* performances was the noted French soprano Gina Cigna (née Juliette Sens). We had done *Faust* together before in Italy, and were later together in *Turandot*. This fine artist sang at the Met for a time, then returned to Europe, and for years has been Directress of "La Scuola di Perfezionamento de LaScala" in Milan.

In Italy, theatrical performances rarely begin until 9:00 P.M.; that causes getting home to be after midnight, even later for a long opera with ballet like *Faust*. The management of the Arena that summer, Maria and Giovanni Zenatello, had spared no cost in getting the best: they had engaged the entire LaScala Ballet for *Faust's* classic dancing and moved the dancers *in toto* by bus from Milan to Verona. The dancing of the group was thrilling under the tutelage of Toscanini's daughter-in-law, Cia Fornaroli, who served also as the group's soloist. The management had also procured the services of the best stage director, the most noted scenery painter, and the most outstanding lighting engineers, all of them with little to do in the summer months and therefore willing to work at more nominal fees.

The membership of the orchestra was a small edition of the United Nations, but only after the local Fascist Society had satisfied itself that at least 51 per cent of all the players were Italian *and* Fascist. (That was paramount in those days.) The nationalities of the remaining 49 per cent of the orchestra players could be anything. Tears sometimes flowed when a fine key player was rejected because he was not Italian *or* Fascist. Summer being desert months in the opera house the world over, each of these fine stage artisans seemed to try to outdo his theatrical colleagues by introducing something individually new, even daring; for example, in the Kermesse Scene of *Faust's* Act II, the scene began with almost no one visible. But little by little, peasants appeared, seemingly walking out of the walls of the sets, until, when the united chorus came there were some 150 persons on the stage to sing those melodies which everyone knows. Another innovation came at the close of the opera when Mefisto is condemned to eternal punishment: a one-person elevator (lift) was installed so that when the time came for Mefisto to take up residence in the hot place, Pinza took his stand on the elevator's floorboard, signaled the operator under the stage, and PFUIT—he disappeared! With Marguerite having expired only moments before the final chorus, the tenor was left to his own ideas. In keeping with what Goethe had in mind, and with the set-up and the dimness of the stage, it seemed right for me to kneel over my beloved's dead body and let that beautiful choral music be heard rather than to distract the audience by moving about as a ghostly shadow, which is usually done when *Faust* is presented in an opera house.

On opening night with those 26,000 persons in the Arena, and more outside, our performance of *Faust* had moved more or less well until the final scene. My Marguerite, Gina Cigna, and I had agreed to do as little acting as possible in the final scene since, in the story, Faust is stricken with remorse at the death of his beloved. Came the closing chorus that night, and as I was preparing to kneel beside Marguerite's dead body, in the darkness of the stage, I accidentally stepped on the index finger of Gina Cigna's left hand and felt it give clear through my shoe sole. And she, poor lady, had to lie still (being supposedly dead) until the final orchestral chord had been played. I cannot say who suffered more: she, with the physical agony of a mashed finger, or I, with psychological knots-in-the-stomach and nothing to do but kneel and wait. "The show must go on!"

During the 1934–35 season, the Opera of Chicago featured Joseph Benton in eleven performances of eight operas: *Faust*, *La Bohème*, *La Traviata*, *Madama Butterfly*, *Manon*, *Marta*, *Rigoletto*, and *Tosca*. This photograph, taken for the opera company, appeared frequently in newspapers, programs, billboards, and other opera publicity.

Joseph Benton, as costumed for the role of the Duke in Verdi's *Rigoletto*, a role which he performed many times with such companies as the Metropolitan Opera, Opera of Chicago, Muny Opera of Cincinnati, and in many leading houses throughout Europe. The stage jewelry worn with this costume was once owned by the Czarina of Russia.

Rodolfo, the poet in Puccini's *La Bohème*, was a favorite role of Benton's, one that he created more than one hundred and fifty times.

Joseph Benton, as Pinkerton in Puccini's *Madama Butterfly* in Milan, Italy, 1929. The cast included the renowned soprano, Rosetta Pampanini.

This photograph of Joseph Benton was taken by the New York *Times* especially for his debut in Massenet's *Manon* at the Metropolitan Opera in 1936.

Always the poet, Joseph Benton here creates the role of Julien in Charpentier's *Louise* for the Opera of Chicago (1936). The title role was sung by the beautiful soprano, Helen Jepson.

"O Romeo, Romeo! wherefore art thou Romeo...?" Joseph Benton, as costumed in deep shades of green for a performance of Gounod's *Romeo et Juliette* at the Paris Opera in 1931.

Smetana's *The Bartered Bride* was performed in English before sell-out audiences in St. Louis in 1937 with Suzanne Fischer, and in Chicago in 1939 with Hilda Burke. The costume was especially ordered from Czechoslovakia for these performances.

Joseph Benton, as he appeared in his debut at the Metropolitan Opera, in Act III of Massenet's *Manon*, with Lucrezia Bori, one of the world's greatest interpreters of the role (1936).

The 1931 season in Cairo, Egypt, allowed time for sightseeing. Joseph Benton is pictured at the Temple of Komombo (above), and before the Sphinx (below) with soprano Tatiana Menotti (near Cairo).

This photograph was taken by a Milan photographer for Benton's debut in Italy in Verdi's *La Traviata*, Act I (1928).

Joseph Benton made a convincing British Army officer stationed in India, as he appeared, along with soprano Lily Pons, in Delibes' *Lakmé* at the Metropolitan Opera (1936) and the Opera of Chicago (1935). This photograph accompanied a feature story in the New York *Times* in 1936.

In 1936, the Metropolitan Opera mounted the first performance ever in English of Puccini's *Gianni Schicchi*. The leading roles were sung by Joseph Benton, Hilda Burke, and Lawrence Tibbett.

Joseph Benton, as costumed for Lionello, the country boy, in von Flotow's *Marta*.

The Opera of Chicago presented, in 1935, the American premiere (also the first in the Western Hemisphere) of Respighi's *La Fiamma (The Flame)*. The performances, which featured Joseph Benton and soprano Rosa Raisa, received world-wide acclaim.

The Oklahoma Tenor.

Leading Role in a World Premiere

The human touch is valuable in opera singing as well as in most other endeavors of life, not to mention the power of personality and the ability to say "no" when necessary. Elsewhere mention is made about two Catholic priests whose human touch and encouragement did much for the advancement of my career in Italy. They were: (1) The PFC (Private First Class) priest of the small church in Voghera and (2) "Top Sergeant" Don Licinio Refice of Rome, whose opera *Cecilia* was given in the Royal Opera House in Rome in eight thrilling performances. It was his wish that I be the tenor.

In the history of the earliest Christian Church, it is generally agreed that the first woman ever to accept Christianity was the Roman aristocrat, Cecilia, who later on is counted as one of the Saints as well as the patroness of music. She is often shown in pictures seated at a Roman organ and accompanying a choir of angels singing in the background. So vibrant was Cecilia's faith in real life that she persuaded her husband,

Valeriano, to become also a follower of the Man from Galilee. Such is the story of Don Licinio Refice's opera *Cecilia*.

My first three performances that year at the Royal Opera House in Rome (Il Teatro Reale dell'Opera) were in the title role of Giordano's opera *Andrea Chénier*, replacing Beniamino Gigli who had commitments elsewhere. After three performances with a stellar cast consisting of Rosetta Pampanini, Mario Basiola, Giuseppina Sani, Giacomo Vaghi, and Maestro Edouardo Vitali, I was withdrawn from the active list and put to rehearsing *Cecilia* for its world premiere.

Now, *Cecilia* is a composition of the then "modern" school, music of such shifting harmonizations as its newness fathered in 1934. It was not accepted by every son of operatic Italy. Don Licinio attended practically all of the rehearsals of his opera and was constantly urging all of us of the cast to "sing lightly" ("cantar leggermente") on the frequent phrases bristling with harmonic sandburs lest during a public performance, especially during a first-ever giving of the work, it be hissed or even whistled—which is still worse and spells rigor mortis for any opera in Italy, at least for one entire generation.

The cost of staging a new operatic work is colossal. Everything has to be new: scenery, sets, make-up, costumes, even the manuscript services of music copyists who make needed changes in the already-printed orchestration. The quality of all divisions of the mounting of *Cecilia* was the highest, and costumes for us soloists were of excellent taste. There were three costumes for the tenor, Valeriano: an at-home two-piece suit, a rough purple wool or "street toga," and a dress-up toga and boots of gold leather with cape of cherry-red silk, embroidered in olive-green for the span of a wide selvage. The costumes of the leading soprano (Claudia Muzio) and the baritone (Carmelo Maugeri) were also handsome and in correct historical taste.

It seemed strange to me that during all of the rehearsals for the new opera, social life continued unabatedly. One reason was that the personal touch can be cashed in at the box office. The management of the opera house, in fact, wrote us soloists please to accept as many invitations as we could handle. I found myself accepting invitations to luncheons, teas, dinners, and after-rehearsal buffets in the homes of almost strangers. All, however, were socially delightful. Some of these invitations I was able to cope with by exchanging courtesies and giving a dinner in turn at the Hotel Quirinale where I was stopping. This was all in accordance with "When in Rome be romantic." Great fun as long as it lasted.

In the fragile story of *Cecilia* there is little scenic action; in fact, we had to invent action. In the scene depicting the husband's (Valeriano's) conversion to Christianity through Cecilia's fine life and gentle ministrations, there is, toward the end of the act, an orchestral passage of protracted length which depicts her husband's mental transformation and resolution to become also a follower of Christ. The scene takes place in the couple's home: Cecilia draped upon a handsome *chaise lounge* while Valeriano, her husband, sits on a rug of goats' hair on the floor, his head in his wife's lap as he gazes soulfully into her eyes.

Now, when one sings opera in any land, one is expected naturally to converse in the language of that country; so it was that during our rehearsals of *Cecilia* in Rome, every one of the cast spoke Italian to each other. This is as it should have been. Came the seventh performance and that static-acting scene: Madame Muzio draped herself upon the *chaise lounge*, I beside it on the rug of goat's hair, my head on her lap, my eyes gazing soulfully into hers. (Never before in any of the preceding six performances of the opera did I ever get tickled, but the night of this seventh performance I did. I stifled the amusement instantly.) Just then and without moving her lips Madame Muzio said to me in the most perfect English, "Dull, isn't it?!" I was so suddenly surprised that I forgot to be tickled. At the end of the act, I went to her dressing room and asked in my best Oklahoma English where she learned such accent-free English. Her answer was, "Silly boy! The first years of my school life were spent in a convent just outside of London where my father was chorus master at Covent Garden Opera House, so I was speaking English before you were—and what about my eleven years with the Chicago Opera?" She autographed and gave to me one of the fine photographs of herself as Cecilia. It hangs in my home in Norman now. Its dedication?—written in English!

Royal Opera of Cairo

During the 1920's and the 1930's, there were two seasons of opera booked from Milan, that were sought after and auditioned for by most singers because of the seasons' decided prestige, artistic quality, and solid financial worth. These two seasons were those in Holland and Egypt, each subsidized by that country's Ministry of the Arts. It was indeed a boost to the old morale to be one of the three tenors selected for the Italian opera season of 1931 in Egypt and 1933 in Holland.

By far the most powerful office for managing opera in Italy in those days was that of Emilio Ferone and Associates of Milan. He controlled the careers of the greatest singers of that time, and never too pleasantly, either. You were a nobody until Ferone smelled money and got interested in you; then you became Mr. Big and could strut your stuff along with the best of them (with reason or without). In both of the opera seasons in Cairo and Holland, Ferone was the king-pin, the "Big Me, Little You" man. He somehow managed to get to both the Cairo season and the one in Holland at some period, but just when he might be in the audience (and unknown to the cast on stage), one could never tell. Such uncertainty made for a truly good performance.

Verdi was approaching sixty when he decided to write *Aida*. The idea for this opera first came about when the Khedive of Egypt wanted some fitting spectacle to crown the international excitement of the opening of the Suez Canal in 1869. The Royal Opera House in Cairo was new that year also. The Khedive wanted an opera based on an Egyptian story and with a like cast of characters. Verdi was not a fly-by-night composer who could grind out tunes at will, and he had many commitments in those years to take care of both at home and outside. Moreover, he could not find a libretto which suited him, so the new opera was not ready when the canal and the opera house were. Not until Christmas Eve of 1871 did the world get to hear *Aida*, its most operatic opera.

The idea of giving the new Egyptian opera with the Sphinx and the Pyramids as part of the background scenery was considered, but this had to be given up because of the "Ghiblee" or wind from the desert which stops most normal activities during its annual visit. So it was that the first giving of *Aida* was, after all, in the Royal Opera House in downtown Cairo.

Whenever speaking of opera in Egypt, one is prone to recall that Verdi never heard the opening performance of his *Aida* because of his fear of the sea. In later years he could, of course, have made the trip overland by means of the luxury train, the Orient Express, or today by air. Fortunately there were no water phobias among those of us making the trip from Italy in the 1931 edition of opera in Egypt. Like our sea trip to Tripoli in 1928, the one to Cairo in 1931 filled an entire ship (348 persons). Like most of the others who had Milan as headquarters, I got on the ship at Genoa; others boarded at

Naples. All were in rare good humor. With such a heavily laden ship, the trip to Alexandria in those days required five days; our transportation from Alexandria to Cairo was by means of a special train on the Egyptian State Railway.

I found lodging at the Metropolitan Hotel, a small but first-class hostelry where the clientele was truly international. At that time, Egypt was a protectorate of England's, but English was rarely ever spoken except by those who also subscribed to the British newspapers. In fact, there were more Italians and French in Cairo in those days than there were English. I found the two Italian newspapers published in Cairo superior to any of the others whose language I was able to read. The secretaries in the manager's office of the opera house provided each of us with a list of recommended "safe" restaurants. (One could not be too careful about food in a city of the Near East in those days; germs seemed to walk abroad.)

The Egyptian opera season had been signed with the Milan agency with the understanding that the opening night was to be with an opera new to that part of the world. The opera chosen was *Anima Allegra* (*The Happy Soul*) by Franco Vittadini. It is a charming Puccini-esque opera written with a dash of "*El Sombrero de Tres Picos*" in it. This delightful opera had been given first in 1921 at the Teatro Costanzi in Rome, then in 1923 at the Metropolitan in New York, so it was truly a novelty in Cairo.

The role of Don Pedro in Vittadini's opera *Anima Allegra* was the first one I had to sing in Cairo. Maestro Vittadini lived in his natal city of Pavia which is just south of Milan, a city where I had already sung two seasons, which included various performances of *Lucia* and Perosi's oratorio *The Resurrection of Christ* (given in the eleventh-century Cathedral), both seasons under the good maestro's direction. After learning the role musically, I had studied the opera with him in his home. Such pleasant remembrances.

The sets, stage furniture, and costumes, all of historic Spanish style, had been brought on loan from Rome's Teatro Costanzi (under the Fascists called the Royal Opera House). The costumes were lavish; my own suited my style perfectly, and I felt a lift as soon as I put on either of the two costumes which the tenor wears in this opera. This exuberance evidently was reflected in my singing, because the critiques were unanimously excellent, and each of the five performances of this opera was reviewed in the local newspapers, something out of the ordinary for repeat performances, so we were told.

Standing artistically and financially behind this subsidized season was a family named Baehler. Originally from Switzerland, they owned or controlled in 1931 most of the deluxe hotels of Egypt, and the Baehler villa was one of the show places of Cairo. Since Cairo is the head city of the Mohammedan religion, one was constantly seeing in parks and along streets visitors in bizarre costumes, convention delegates mostly who had come there from the ends of the earth. Arabic was understood by most Egyptians, but if you did not speak Arabic (and you don't unless you were born and reared there), you had to speak French, despite the boast by Britain that Egypt was a British Protectorate. The bulldog tenacity with which the French language held these people stemmed from Napoleon's decision to make of Egypt "la Nouvelle France." He almost did too.

International society in Cairo was abuzz for weeks before the opening of the opera season, and every social climber of the city, from Madame Popgirdle to Betty Bigbelch, outdid herself planning and executing social events. To some of these events we opera singers were invited, too.

ROYAL OPERA OF CAIRO

The publicity regarding the opera's opening was surprisingly diffused. Even the city's street cars and taxis carried streamers telling in Arabic, French, English (how generous!), Greek, and a pair of local *patois* of what, when, where, and how much. Formal white tie was required in all boxes, parquets, and main-floor seats. Only the top two balconies admitted those wearing comfortable clothing, those who really knew opera and were vocal about it. We of the cast of the new opera had rehearsed consistently for eleven days. Madame Baehler had heard snatches of our long rehearsals and seemed to sense the great success which the new opera was going to have in Cairo, so she organized for the cast an after-the-opera buffet at the Semiramis Hotel, one of the world's finest and most luxurious inns. The party lasted (no booze either) until the morning newspapers appeared with detailed accounts of the artistic success of the opera season's opener. (How true is the meaning of the old adage: "We appreciate being appreciated.")

Madame Baehler's pet philanthropy was her Orphanage for Arab Children which she fought for in no uncertain terms; and since many Cairo businessmen and corporations owed her husband money, whenever her "invitation" to them came to contribute or to buy blocks of tickets, they were constrained to "divvy up." So great was Madame Baehler's job in the season's opening opera that when she bought out the house for a last-performance-of-the-season benefit for her orphanage, the cheapest seat was $25.00, every seat was taken, and the benefit was a great success. We of the cast contributed our fee as our gift to the worthy cause.

My Milan-signed contract stated that I would have a list of thirteen performances of six different operas to do during the Cairo season, each one at the same nice fee. We had been in

Cairo only a short time when Pedro Mirassou, one of the three tenors, fell ill of an infected knee and for weeks he was in the Italian Hospital with a case of blood poisoning, caused by the bite of an insect plus infection afterward. "The show must go on," so I was called in to do both his work and my own. The result was that at the end of the season I had done thirty-two performances instead of thirteen of six different operas, and each at a goodly sum.

The International Law Courts were meeting in Cairo during the time of our opera season in the city. This was an auspicious time for Madame Baehler to give one of her fundraising dinners in favor of her Arab orphans. She requested a mixed quartet of singers from the Opera House to give an after-dinner program. I was selected as the tenor of the quartet. We rehearsed and gave quite an acceptable program, mostly of operatic selections. The dinner was held in the home of Sedky Pascià, Prime Minister of Egypt. His villa, across the Nile from one of the chic residential sections of the city, was one of the things-to-see by day or by night in Cairo. The limousine of the Prime Minister collected us at our stopping places and took us to and from the Prime Minister's villa. It was all very elegant save for one event.

The opening number of this program was the Quartet from Flotow's opera *Marta*. It went well. The second number was the duet for soprano and mezzo from the first act of Puccini's *Madama Butterfly*. In that French-style villa there was no room assigned as headquarters for the musicians, so while the two ladies of the quartet were singing their duet, the baritone (Luigi Borgonuovo) and I wandered down the long hall where, from the windows, one had a fine view of the illuminated formal garden and glimpses of the Nile far beyond. We could also observe the reactions of the invited guests, also see and hear the tittering of the Prime Minister's harem—four fat, over-dressed women who through social custom were not permitted to sit among the guests but, wanting to hear the music, had hidden themselves behind tall potted palms. (Since the Arab idea of female beauty is female blubber, these four monstrosities of Sidky Pascià's harem must have been considered ravishing.)

Borgonuovo and I had no idea that we were being watched. Too, our deportment was far from correct as our innocent gestures to each other and facial smirks must have shown. All at once a huge eunuch in prescribed livery appeared, grabbed me by both shoulders and shoved me bruskly outdoors, muttering in Arabic a sort of chant as he did so. In my limping French I asked him why this treatment. Floods of Arabic were his answer. Suddenly I became angry that such treatment should be accorded those who were giving gratis of their talent toward the satisfaction of a selfish politician, and I made this pitiful creature understand that I wanted to speak to the Prime Minister himself, otherwise the remainder of the music program would not be given.

This unpleasant disturbance brought forth the Prime Minister himself as host. After he apologized in polished French, we collected our wits and finished the program. At the reception following the program, several different members of the International Law Courts and their wives expressed chagrin at the way the affair had been handled. Borgonuovo and I were wrong, of course, to laugh at and to point at those harem fatties, not knowing that we were being watched; but physical violence never cured any such sort of misdemeanor.

Looking back upon the entire episode, it is rather amusing to realize how, for a few moments, a mere Okie was receiving the bows and scrapes of the Prime Minister of Egypt.

The Little, Old, Gray Home

(Translation from the French of Robert de Flers' poem, set to music by Massager in his comic opera *Fortunio*.)

I love the little old gray house
Where I grew up near mother's knee;
The days there slipped by like a dream,
In the shade of an old walnut tree.

All things there to me are so dear,
They seem of myself each a part,
For even the ivy that grew round the door
Has entangled itself with my heart.

Alas, my path has strayed away,
Far from such scenes now must I roam;
Yet never from my heart will fade away
The memory of my childhood's happy home.

Knowing Jean de Reszke

"The world's greatest so-and-so," "the so-and-so-est in the country," "there is no greater so-and-so in existence." All of these are typically American superlatives with which we are daily familiar and which follow us in our conversations wherever we go, whether in the workaday world, at a party of friends, or even in the supposed sanctity of our own abode. Indeed, our daily life continues literally to drip with superlatives.

When, however, it comes to discussing opera singers of the past and present, just as with scientists, the superlative mode boils down to a comparative few persons: who was superlative for interpretation, who for histrionics, who for clarity of word-in-song, who "lived" expressively his or her role. Each of these sub-titles opens up a wide door toward a more detailed and personal preference of the speaker. Just as who prefers whom in politics. But through those who heard him in person and those who have so eloquently consigned to paper their thoughts regarding the matter, we are assailed with an almost-unanimous opinion that in the realm of operatic tenors of the latter half of the nineteenth century, it was Jean de Reszke who outdid all of the professional singers of his time, and in a knightly manner so fitting for the Victorianism of the period that his abilities and the times in which he lived went together like the proverbial hand-in-glove. Given the changes of the present time as acted out on the stage for us, being assailed with the correctness of his manner, de Reszke's aristocratic ways might fall flat. But in his day, what he did had never been done before on the stage, and the histrionic grand manner had never before been used. He used it judiciously and made a world-wide personal and stage success of it all.

For the first years of his life as a professional singer, Jean de Reszke sang as a baritone and with good success (Figaro, Valentine, etc.), but he aspired for greater operatic responsibilities, wider acclaim, so he withdrew from the opera stage for a time and studied to sing as a tenor. From then on his success widened yearly. He even learned German, then thought to be an unsingable language, in order to sing Wagner's operas in their original tongue.

Jean de Reszke's wife was French, Marie de Beauharnais, the step-grand niece of Napoleon's first wife's husband, and it was she who helped her husband learn his extended operatic repertoire. As one of his pupils, I got to know Madame de Reszke quite well. She was one of the few French women I have known who had no accent when she spoke English.

After Jean de Reszke sang no more publicly (1902), he taught singing in Paris. But the winters of Paris are cold and damp, so the de Reszke ménage moved to the south of France and settled in Nice where they acquired the villa at 208 Avenue de France, a villa originally built by a wealthy American. It was there that we students of de Reszke had our lessons in the huge studio adjoining the terrace, both of which looked out upon the Mediterranean Sea. All lesson details were presided over by Louis Vachet, de Reszke's secretary, who in professional days had been his valet and confidant. The villa was one of the most handsome of the entire French Riviera and commanded a view out over the Bay of the Angles which was truly impressive. On one occasion we stood on the villa's front porch and watched the entire Submarine Division of the French Navy do its maneuvers within the confines of that sweeping expanse of water. Diving in even the largest submarines is possible because of the depth of the sea near the shore along that stretch of the Mediterranean.

So vast were de Reszke's contacts with world-famous persons in the fields of music and politics that when you went to your lesson at the villa, you never knew who might be already sitting in the beautiful studio waiting to hear your lesson. Thus it was that I met the Grand Duchess Alexandria of Russia, Mary Garden, Reynaldo Hahn (the composer-conductor with whom later I did Mozart's *Don Giovanni* at Cannes, France), John McCormack,* Geraldine Farrar, Nöel Coward, and others. For years de Reszke had wanted to present publicly a "perfect" performance of Mozart's *Don Giovanni* using students in the various roles. The talents of the pupils during the fall and winter terms that year seemed better than usual, so it was decided to give the production that year (1924). My part therein was the role of Don Ottavio.

* John McCormack speaks about "Tenor Bentonelli" on Side C of *John McCormack in Opera & Song* (between "Sweet Hour of Prayer" and "So do I love you," Division "C," ASCO Records, A-110, Monaural.)

At that time I knew no Italian, but I learned the role by rote, thanks to the careful coaching of Madame de Reszke and her niece-in-law, Minia de Reszke, who spoke all languages fluently, it seemed. (Minia was the daughter of Jean's brother, Edouard, the famous basso.) After countless rehearsals, in November of 1924, we presented Mozart's opera at the Casino des Variétés in Nice. So great was its success that we gave it also at Cannes at the Municipal Casino under the direction of Raynaldo Hahn, also at the Opera House in Nice, all three performances with great success. Even de Reszke was pleased.

But the tension of the extra rehearsals, especially those at night, extra lessons, the lack of ability to sleep at night, all told on de Reszke's health. He slumped. On April 3, 1925, he died. All of Nice went into sudden mourning. I was one of the great man's pupils asked to sit up with the body the night before the funeral. Hours thus spent are long, and since there were so many flowers sent and exposed on the floor around the coffin in the studio where we all had taken our lessons in months past, I made a list of some of the donors of floral offerings. They included remembrances from the King and Queen of England, Winston Churchill, Lloyd George and family, the President of France (M. LeBlanc), the Grand Duchess Alexandria of Russia, pianist Ignace Jan Paderewski (de Reszke's fellow-countryman), President Woodrow Wilson, and a long list of persons whose names did not ring a bell with me. The next day, after a sizable funeral cortège in downtown Nice, the reading of the High Funeral Mass took place in the handsome old Cathedral of Nice, which was packed in every cranny with standees. All of us pupils attended in a body.

The cortège moved from the Nice Cathedral to the railway station where the coffin was taken by rail to Paris and interment at the Cemetery of Montparnasse quite near the graves of some of the greatest men and women whom France has ever produced.

Jean de Reszke was a great man personally and taught us, his pupils, much more than just singing. He was the true internationalist and citizen of the world. He gave when it was required, but when not required, it was his counsel that usually avoided a complication. He touched our lives and each one of us, his pupils, has been stronger therefore.

Love Was a Little Thing

*Cover the harp with dust,
Silence each singing string,
Bury all hope, all trust—
Love was a little thing.*

*Bury so deep no gust
Of a stray wind may bring
Memories deep with rust—
Love was a little thing.*

The Assuan Dam, 1931

Photography has always interested me. The first camera I ever owned was a box camera made by Eastman which cost me the salary of two Saturdays clerking in the Red Front Store in my home town of Sayre, Oklahoma, that being the munificent sum of $3.00, by mail and postpaid. It took excellent pictures, too. After that box camera got stepped on there came a line of ever-better ones and my arrival in Cairo, Egypt, with the opera company was with a deluxe model of the vest-pocket Kodak. But, I reasoned, in this ancient land where each part is a "happy hunting ground" for all those who take pictures, it is impossible to take adequate landscapes because of the immensity of the objects being photographed along with the smallness of the vest-pocket Kodak. So, I bought a fine "pull-out" Kodak with Zeiss lens, the kind that professionals used and were proud of. I still have that camera. It has been a long-time and true friend. So also has been the manager of the Eastman Agency in Cairo where I bought that "pull-out" camera, Mr. Hratch Kalfayan, a Cairo-Armenian now living in Canada with his family.

Mention has been made of Egypt's being the land of strange illnesses and virus infections, and of how one of our 1931 company's three tenors, Pedro Mirassou, fell victim to one of these mysterious infections soon after our arrival. He spent almost five weeks in the Italian Hospital of Cairo, fighting a deep abcess on his left knee, which grew angry from only a small scratch. His wife was sent for, and for a time, in spite of excellent care, it was not known if he would live or not. Being one of our company's two dramatic tenors, several heavy operas awaited his return to the opera house. In the meantime, the other dramatic tenor, Giovanni Voyer, and I had to carry on because the season was subsidized by the government and all performances had been sold through subscription and season tickets. Too, since both Voyer and I were paid per performance, "the more the merrier" for each of us. The agenda at one time was such that in fourteen days I sang nine performances of four different operas of which seven were on successive evenings. I never felt better, healthwise.

So it was that when Mirassou was able to return to his roles, Voyer and I were practically idle, having said our piece and done our do. After the list of operas for the remainder of the season was announced, I decided that I would turn tourist and visit some of the historic places in Egypt rather than sit around with my teeth in my mouth and have little or even less to do, provided, of course, that I could get the management's permission in writing for me to be absent for those almost two weeks. I wrote out my own petition and, wonder of wonders, it was granted. The only proviso was that each evening I would send a telegram to the management in Cairo

THE ASSUAN DAM

as to where I could be reached by telegram or telephone on the following day. Fair enough.

The Kalfayans took me with my luggage to the station to catch the southbound night train, and the next day about 2:00 P.M. my Pullman roomette looked out upon Assuan and its mud-caked laborers visible wherever one might be. And although it was only the first of March, the desert heat was making its presence felt. Like any other tourist, I was taken on guided trips through the intricacies of the Assuan Dam, making the distance from one end of it to the other, which is well over a mile, in a fine Russian bus heavy with stainless-steel ornamentation (policy!). We were told that the original Assuan Dam was completed in 1902 and that this 1931 addition, upward of seven meters, would deepen the great lake that the original caused to back up behind itself, and would permit the irrigation of several more million acres of desert. At the close of our fourth tour in, around, and through the dam, a band of savage-looking Bedouins danced for us, and one of the snapshots I took of their dancing shows one old boy seemingly suspended in mid-air.

On the third day I boarded a passenger boat on the Nile for the return trip from Assuan to Cairo. My passage had been booked before leaving Cairo, and my stateroom was the choicest of them all. It was located in the boat's middle, complete with covered small porch to one side and a real bathroom. We ten passengers took our meals at one long table in the front part, and the food served was excellent—international menu, but leaning heavily toward French cuisine. And again French was the official language.

The trip down the Nile by boat was well organized, as tourist trips go. True to my promise, each evening, when the group of passengers returned to the boat from sightseeing, I would send the opera management in Cairo (Maestro Parenti) a telegram saying where it would be possible to contact me the following day if needed. We visited the ruins of Luxor, Karnak, Thebes, Edfu, Kom-ombo, and the then recently-discovered tomb of Nifertiti; also Saqqara and Abú-Simbel, as well as the Valley of the Kings and the tomb of Tut-ank-amen, the contents of whose tomb are today on display in the Museum of Egyptian Culture in Cairo. Each day was a new and thrilling experience for us boat-travelers.

We had been, for the day, in the Valley of the Kings and had started back to the boat when, sure enough, here came the son of the dragoman of our boat, plodding across the dunes and waving a blue telegram. It was for me and from Maestro Pilogatti of the Cairo opera management, saying that the following Sunday (this was on Friday late afternoon) I would be singing in the matinee performance and not to fail. For some strange reason he did not say in what opera I was expected to appear.

Aboard the boat again I squared finances with the purser, wired Cairo that I would be there, got help with my luggage, and took the 7:30 P.M. train for Cairo. No time for supper and little time for sleep, too, with the train stopping at every mud village along the way; but at least I was lying prone and that helps greatly.

Upon arrival in Cairo, I did not go to my hotel at once, but took a taxi to the opera house—it was then 10:30 on Sunday morning, and from the posters outside the opera house, I saw that I was to sing in *Madama Butterfly* with Rosetta Pampanini. (This opera was not scheduled for Cairo in 1931, although she and I had done the opera together in various editions throughout Italy in previous years, also *Adriana Lecouvreur* and *Traviata*.) However, uncertainty is a dreadful state of mind and can make you sick at heart. The matinee of *Butterfly* that day went perfectly, and we received equally as many curtain calls as when we did that opera for the first time together.

Our opera season in Cairo ground to a successful ending. We had made many local friends, chief among them for me being the Kalfayans, the Baehler families, and some members of the season's board of directors. Madame Baehler invited all of us to a formal dinner the night that the season closed. It was held at the Hotel Semiramis, which the Baehler Corporation owned. The sight of the full moon rising out of the Nile as we sat down to a sumptuous midnight dinner is something that I have always remembered. The following morning, we entrained for Alexandria-by-the-Sea where we gave one performance (*Tosca*), then took the boat for Catania, Naples, and Genoa.

Other than friendships made and the trip I had by boat on the Nile to visit the great ruins of past centuries, I think that the most memorable incident that year was seeing how the stage of the opera house in Cairo had been braced and supported by large pillars and arches of both stone and wood to bear the extra weight of the wild animals which were brought onto the stage for the Triumphal March at the first-anywhere giving of Verdi's opera *Aida* (1871).

La vie est vaine;	*Le vie est brève;*	*La vie est telle*
Un peu d'amour	*Un peu d'espoir*	*Que Dieu la fit;*
Un peu de haine	*Un peu de neve*	*Et telle qu'elle*
Et puis bonjour.	*Et puis bonsoir.*	*Elle suffit.*

Spirit's Retrospect

*Full many a crescent moon has waxed and waned
Since first the shaggy turf was broke for me;
Full many a hopeful Spring has passed away
Since first I Icame to begin my stay
Beneath this wind-blown, jagged tree
Where drouthy Summer parches, thirsty-stained.*

*And as I pass the years (without a ray
In my forgotten house with sunken wings
Where all is dark and clammy-cold
As my own spent body's sickly mould),
I have a chance to think upon the things
That during Life were want to slip away*

*From out my grasp: Joy, Love and Beauty; even Truth
Took wings and fled to lands beyond my rushing, earthly race.
But now, with rested vision, clearer eyes,
I value fully four segments of Life's prize:
The swish of falling rain; the tides; blank space;
And the too-swift passing of the time called Youth.*

The Rolex

When, at seventeen years of age, we left the farm to move to the University of Oklahoma town of Norman for me to attend the University, my father bought me my first watch. It was a wrist watch and it cost $4.98, but its makers were evidently so ashamed of its lack of pedigree that they refused to give it any name at all. It lost over an hour of time each day, and since I was living in a different town from the one where the watch had been bought, the second town's jeweler refused to adjust the watch without payment each time I took it to his shop. (The charge he made was twenty-five cents for each adjustment, the wage in those days of one-fourth of a day's manual labor.) I did not take it very often to be adjusted.

Years later, I enjoyed a financially successful season in Cairo, Egypt, especially successful owing to my doubling the number of performances sung after the illness of one of our other tenors (discussed earlier). In those days, it was possible to send money out of the country without the strict formalities of today. So it was that I sent to my father in Oklahoma several thousand dollars through the National Bank of Egypt to be put on time-deposit (called "Certificate of Deposit" today), in our Norman bank.

The following summer (1931), I went for a time to Switzerland to get away from the blistering heat of Italy, and from Zurich, made a special trip to Neuchatel where the Longine watch factory is located. There I changed some of the money from those extra performances of opera in Egypt into the finest Rolex wrist watch which Longine made at that time. And, knowing the way that such articles disappear, especially backstage in the opera house, I had my name engraved across the back of the watch in bold, aggressive letters. It was early for such a timepiece to be known outside of Switzerland since that Rolex model was new that summer. My acquisition was the cynosure of all eyes among my Italian friends. I even wore it on stage for reasons of safety rather than leave it in the dressing room. I wore it as a laugh on the stocking of my right knee in the third act of Massenet's *Manon* and Gounod's *Roméo et Juliette*. The gold chain-bracelet added to the glitter of the costume and also helped to reveal the effete weakness of nature which was the moving essence of the lack of character of *des Grieux*.

The years passed, and during them all, the Rolex wrist watch was my constant companion; however, I did have to buy a pocket watch, a Hamilton, to wear with formal apparel in the United States. For some twenty years the wrist watch did not have to visit the repairman except for its yearly cleaning. Of course I respected the delicate balance of the watch's insides and always took it off completely whenever engaged in some form of activity which might jerk its insides, like playing noisesome piano accompaniments, lifting a heavily filled valise, or (since I wear the watch on my right wrist)

THE ROLEX

shaking hands with after-the-performance stage-Johnnies, some of whom even today seem to think the only cordial handshakes are those that cause an audible crunching of the bones.

During the summer of 1972, this notable watch had to have major repairs because wear had consumed its hairspring. A local representative of the Longine Company sent the watch to its American sub-factory, but they had no repair parts that would fit. So they sent the watch to Switzerland where the makers redid it completely despite its being a model of 1931, then sent it back to Norman, and the cost was nothing at all. It is through treatment like that that the Swiss have maintained their reputation for integrity and honesty in business throughout the centuries. Would that other people were as honest and their handiwork as genuine as those who made my Rolex watch!

—Warning—

*If poet be gone
Then thot is dead,
And what is Life
With thots unsaid?*

*When thots are said,
The mind leaps up
Like fragment wine
Within the cup;
It spreads its wings
And soars afar
To myriad lands
Where old kings are.*

*If singer be gone,
The song is mute;
And who can sing
From a dusty throat?*

*So let there be poets
That thots may be freed;
And let there be singers
That nations take heed.*

A Hug from Tosca

During the 1930's there was an outstanding soprano who specialized in singing the title role of Puccini's opera *Tosca*. She sang other roles too, but *Tosca* was her specialty. She was a handsome, statuesque blonde given also to repeating in a soft voice some of the foibles and miniature gestures off-stage which the original Tosca possibly did in real life. Backstage, her reputation as a colleague was varied, all of those expressing an opinion agreeing that she could be either friendly when least expected or else otherwise (also when least expected). On different occasions she had sung *Tosca* in London at Covent Garden. That was the only contact she had had with working in an English-speaking country, but it was rumored that she prided herself upon the manner in which she could speak English, including some choice bits of rubber-stamp swear words and worn-out slang popular years before. Her chief linguistic sin was translating into English the word-by-word sequence of some idiom from Mid-Eastern Europe; this turned out more amusing than explanatory.

The first time I ever sang *Tosca* anywhere was in French at the Municipal Opera of Nice. After which it became one of my favorites, and one that I was to perform many times. The Sardou play bristles with blood-and-thunder theatricality, and the music glows with some of Puccini's finest melodic efforts. The translation of the opera's libretto from Italian into French is thrilling both to read and to sing, so it was with anticipation that I found that my agent in Milan had signed for my American debut as Mario Cavaradossi in *Tosca* at the Opera of Chicago (1934), and with that soprano so famous as the interpreter of the title role of that opera. I had done fifty-six performances of the opera in Italian in Italy, Yugoslavia, Egypt, and Tripoli, so I had a sure grip on my role before the Chicago debut in my native land came along.

It was thrilling to be at home again, also to be one of the first Americans to sing at that no-expense-spared opera house at 20 North Wacker Drive in Chicago. (Mr. Insull's "insulation" was truly great!) Our rehearsals were adequate, but during them all the famous lady from Eastern Europe insisted upon speaking her own brand of English to me, while with the other members of the cast and with Maestro Gennaro Papi, she spoke in far better Italian. This gave me the feeling of being patronized, of being made fun of in my own native land. I spoke with the lady in ANY language as little as possible. She glared back at me through a cynical smile. At the dress rehearsal of *Tosca*, the huge auditorium of the opera house was sprinkled with newsmen and photographers, several of whom afterward interviewed various members of the cast. I was careful to be noncommittal regarding the following day's debut.

In my long experience I have learned that the American public listens to opera with its eyes, not its ears; that if you

A HUG FROM TOSCA

look well and, as a man, are polite but also kindly aggressive on the stage in your acting, poor vocalism and bad musical taste are partly excused by most listeners. Now, *Tosca* is one opera of the Latin repertory in which each interpreter can easily be "kindly aggressive." I had had my costumes made by Giuseppe Noè, costumer at LaScala; they were of gray and green wool and of impeccable good taste. The made-to-order knee-high boots of black patent leather with fair-leather turn-over tops revealed the high social order to which Mario belonged in the actual social life of Rome of the 1840's. Too, for the opening, there was a sold-out house. That always helps the old morale.

In the story of this opera, in the first act, there is a scene in which Tosca, the noted operatic soprano of Rome, is trying to get her sweetie-pie, the portrait painter, Mario Cavaradossi, to come to her villa following her theatrical performance that evening. He debates for a time, then to get rid of her consents to come.

For several pages leading up to this point, the soprano has a short arietta which is melodious and completely fetching. As this arietta developed the evening of the debut, I noticed how tightly my Tosca was holding me. Then it suddenly dawned that this feigned affection was being shown so that she might cut short my breath for the High B♭ which is all-important to the success of the act. (This soprano could not endure a colleague's success, not even in his own native land).

As the time drew near for the high note, so drew tighter the soprano's vise-like hug of my rib-cage. Then this thought came to me: the woman in question had begun her theatrical life as an acrobat in a circus, I as a worker on my father's farm in Western Oklahoma and my physical strength was correspondingly to be respected along with hers. So, stung by her low tactics, I let her have that fortissimo High B♮ only four inches from her right ear. She winced. The audience applauded.

At the end of the act, I swallowed my pride and went to the soprano's dressing room. "You vahs not nize to me yoost now, you sink in my ear," she complained. But she also understood that I had caught on to her ruse of injuring the high note in my debut in my own land so as to add to her own success. In succeeding opera seasons, this soprano and I sang together frequently, not only in *Tosca*, but in Catalani's *Lorelei* and Puccini's *Turandot* as well; but we were always a bit stand off-ish toward each other.

As Lynn Riggs, the University of Oklahoma's noted playwright from whose play *Green Grow The Lilacs* the musical *OKLAHOMA!* was taken, used to put it: "A stitch in time saves two in the bush." So it was with the famous Tosca from Eastern Europe.

Stale Fish In Venice

In 1928, my opera debut was made in Italy as Alfredo in Verdi's *La Traviata* at Faenza. The agent who made possible this debut, Manlio Pasotto, in selling me the bill of goods that I should accept his proposition for a debut, had told me that back of the city in the hills are found deposits of the clay which permit high temperatures in firing the ceramics in high-powered kilns. This makes possible the glaze so sought after by those who know and by those collectors of ceramics who look for quality museum pieces. To have sung in such an artistic city, he said, would be helpful for future bookings. The debut was more or less successful, and soon thereafter, Pasotto came forth with another season in which I might be one of the leading tenors in not one but three operas: *Traviata*, *La Bohème*, and *Lucia*, all at the Malibran Opera House in Venice, the theatre named for the famous Italian contralto of the past century, Maria Malibran.

The year that I arrived on the campus of the University of Oklahoma was the year that Miss Merle Newby resigned as

Assistant Professor of Violin to devote more time to her family in Oklahoma City. I was enrolled in the College of Arts and Sciences, but still heard echoes of the excellence of the violin teaching of Miss Merle Newby (Mrs. Frank Buttram). In 1928, some of the six Buttram children were attending school in Switzerland. I had known the family in Oklahoma before going to Europe to study. Mr. Buttram wrote me in Milan from Switzerland, where he and Mrs. Buttram were visiting their children, to ask if I might be singing somewhere in opera "soon." Having agreed to sing at the Malibran Theatre in Venice as leading tenor in three different operas, I wrote the Buttrams at their hotel in Lucerne, but had no further word from them until the day of the debut when they arrived in Venice. They had traveled by air, then parked their monoplane at Chioggia, the town built upon the last solid rock before leaping off into the doubtfully solid slime-pits of Venice itself.

The dress rehearsal of *La Bohème* on the stage of the Malibran Theatre had been long and taxing, ending about 2:00 A.M., with everyone famished for some hot food. But even in cosmopolitan Venice, restaurants do not keep open all night. After telephoning, however, a "trattoria" was found open and we found the restaurant eventually. One can walk over water-paved Venice if one knows what walkways to take. Fortunately one of our cast members was Venetian and could guide our weary steps.

Unfortunately, the restaurant we found open was not prepared to feed a troop of more than forty persons. It was rather a question of our eating what was available, not what each person might wish to order. Along with others of our group, I ate a bowl of fish soup (*"bouibaisse"*) and some bread-sticks. The fish's freshness was several days past, and it gave all of us who ate it an active set-to of food poisoning. All of the rest of the night at the Hotel Cavaletto, I was sick, sick, sick. The next afternoon, the afternoon of the debut which was to follow that night, I walked to the theatre from the hotel (built in 1440), and as I passed the telephone operator in the theatre's foyer, she called to me that she had had a telephone message for me. A Mr. and Mrs. Impossibly-Spelled-Name had telephoned in English from Chioggia to say that they were to be at the Grand Hotel in Venice and would I please call them there. I knew of no one but the Buttrams who might be doing such, so I telephoned the Grand Hotel, found them and spoke with them. Ptomaine poisoning is never the subject of a happy conversation, especially when it treats of one's singing a major opera role in a foreign land where Americans are disliked even before they utter a mutter. Besides, excuses are for sophomores.

By curtain time that evening, I had gotten rid of most of the stale fish but not the soreness which it had caused, or the weakness. The voice was clear but far too confidential. I asked God for divine guidance and to help me with those beastly middle notes, always the banc of my vocal existence. The performance began. The duet in Act I between the baritone and me went well. This duet, with its several tricky musical entrances and debonnaire acting was then followed by the delightful solos of the soprano and the tenor. The tenor solo of the first act of *La Bohème* contains the most perfectly written High C in all of opera. In spite of my physical weakness, the High C came well and drew prolonged applause from the audience, so long, in fact, that the conductor had to stop and wait for the hand clapping to diminish. I thanked God then, later, and even today for permitting me to sing publicly that test-aria so well at my first singing of the entire opera, and in spite of the antics of that stale fish inside my belly. Also, that the others who had also eaten of that stale fish were able to do their roles in more or less convincing manner despite the same trouble.

When the performance was over, the Buttrams were hosts at a hot buffet of lavish proportions in the Grand Hotel for all of the opera's cast. The following summer in Oklahoma City, the Buttrams were sponsors for a solo recital by me in their palatial home. Their deaths were individual losses to the entire State of Oklahoma. We have too few Buttrams in this naughty old world.

Tuna Fish in a Can

In ancient times, the island of Sicily and all of the southern part of the mainland of Italy proper were the breadbasket of ancient Greece. The principal foodstuffs raised in this region were wheat and other small grains, yet, one must not forget all kinds of grapes and various kinds of food-fish as well. One of the most sought after of all food-fishes was a near-relative of that part of Italy, the "tunny," which we know today as tuna or tuna fish, a delicacy on any table during any period of the year.

Lecce is located in the "heel of the boot," which is Italy on the map, and is some twelve miles from the Adriatic Sea. It is one of the best fishing spots for tuna anywhere. Soon after arriving in Lecce for the rehearsals of that town's opera season, we were shown through the tuna-canning plant. It was fascinating. Only the larger tuna are tinned after being netted, those that weigh from 100 to 150 pounds and, of course, the choice cuts are the steaks, the tenderloin along the backbone; the rest goes for pet food and fertilizer. A certain amount of the steaks are frozen and appear as "fresh" tuna on the menus of fine hotels and restaurants all over Europe. Uncooked tuna is dark blue in color; the fish's belly is blue with speckles of gray. The noted lyric tenor, Tito Schipa, was a native of Lecce and did much to help modernize the packing of tuna for world distribution. With the invention of means to can this fragile food in metal containers, and still later to freeze it artificially, its appearance on more tables has become a reality.

Whenever the Greeks during their halcyon days occupied any country, they brought with them samples of their rich theatrical works, and thus established a new chapter of Greek culture wherever they landed. So it was with the city of Lecce. A sizable theatre had been built during the uncharted centuries of the past, but man's cupidity for already-trimmed building stones, along with a heavy earthquake during the Middle Ages, had just about ruined the theatre. It stood there, a mass of stone rubble.

Tito Schipa (born Raffaele Attilio Amadeo Schipa on January 2, 1889), became not only famous as a tenor and noted opera singer, but also rich as a packer of tinned tuna shipped throughout the world. Aside from his attainments, Schipa had civic pride. He decided to rebuild the Greek Theatre in his home town and to inaugurate its reopening with an opera season. Both the transitory opera season and the more lasting restoration of the ancient building were to be personal gifts to his townspeople, and all of this without his name being used as the donor. The old playhouse from the time of the Greeks was referred to as "il Teatro Greco," not as "il Teatro Schipa." So it was that Schipa, in between his own opera singing all over the world, bought the pile of stone rubble and had workmen set about to restore the utter chaos of the ruins.

For years the stone masons labored to restore the mess that was the town's eye-sore, and there came forth a Greek Theatre worthy of the name. Its inauguration took place in April of 1930 with Schipa himself acting as impresario for the opera season and giving his home-town citizens free tickets to an opera season which presented twenty-two performances of four different operas. My own assignment was as Rodolfo in six performances of Puccini's *La Bohème*. All of the principal singers except me were from LaScala, most of them longtime personal friends of Schipa. The two sopranos were two of the then-reigning queens of song, Rosetta Pampanini and Mafalda Favero. Each performance of each of the four operas was to a full house, and all of the citizenry were genuinely grateful to their home-town boy who made good in opera and and also in the tuna-fish industry. To be sure, they loved him for his unselfishness.

As an extra gift to his townspeople, Schipa decided to present Mascagni's opera *Iris*, since it had not been given in Lecce for a generation. By coincidence, the two sopranos alternating in *La Bohème* were the finest two interpreters of the title role of *Iris* in the entire world of opera. But owing to previous commitments, Rosetta Pampanini could not be free, while Mafalda Favero's schedule could be made elastic for the dates needed for the preparation of this difficult opera. Since I was already there some five hundred miles from my headquarters in Milan, the management asked me to do the tenor role (Osaka). I had heard the opera only once, at LaScala with the fine tenor Aureliano Pertile and the conductor Arturo Toscanini. I had been completely impressed by the performance. I well knew that *Iris* demands a dramatic

OKLAHOMA TENOR

tenor to do it properly, but at Lecce, I was willing to risk my neck to get to do the role, it being so very difficult to put a new role into one's repertory.

I wrote to Giuseppe Noè, noted costumer at LaScala who had made all of my other opera costumes and who had my measurements. He could be trusted to do a fine job of making appropriate costumes in absentia. What he made for me to wear in *Iris* and sent by railway express could not have been improved upon. The organization which we Americans call Chamber of Commerce sold out the house at each of the three performances of *Iris*. Too, this group was host at the reception given following the opening performance of the opera.

The story of *Iris* takes place in Japan in the Middle Era of Oriental history. It is extremely difficult to stage as an opera. Our rehearsals numbered more than we ever had for any other operatic work. Its satisfactions, however, are correspondingly great—provided, of course, you have a cast of soloists who are ready to accept suggestions and a steel-fisted stage manager who makes the cast work together as a unit (like a football team). Imagine how thankful we were for having taken suggestions at those many rehearsals when, to our surprise, about the time that the opera was to begin that opening night, who should enter the opera house and sit in the royal box by invitation of the city's mayor, but the composer of *Iris* himself, Pietro Mascagni. It was a happy evening.

Fearing that the dramatic nature of this tenor music might strain my lyric voice, I never sang *Iris* again after those three performances at Lecce, the tuna-fish capital of Italy.

Sicilian Interlude

It is said that generally you will find Sicilians to be suave, sentimental, romantic, and sincere, but they can also be completely unpleasant, like any other balanced human being. Too, they are the hand kissingest men this side of Rodolfo Valentino. When they are particularly glad to see each other, Sicilians will indulge in a kissing operation that involves both cheeks of both parties; women kiss women, men kiss men, and sometimes they do it with one or more of each. Sicily is a large island, completely overpopulated, and has always been so (too much kissing?). With so many mouths to feed, prices are high and even simple foods expensive. There is not enough food to go around and that is one of the reasons that so many old-time Sicilian families have had to move elsewhere, either to other regions of Italy or to foreign lands. Practically every young person there reportedly has "a cousin in Chicago,"—and doubtless has.

During past ages, the island of Sicily was Classic Greece's breadbasket, wine bottle, and source of wool. As for food of local importance, the Sicilian sauces put on hot cooked pasta are many. It is true that Sicily is full of pasta, and it is therefore inevitable that if you visit the country, you will be, too. Pasta is a mixture of flour, water, and eggs, and it comes in fifty-seven different varieties, each varying with the kind of sauce one drapes over the unflavored, cooked pasta. With grated cheese added as desired, you are now ready for a gastronomic delight. Cheap, too.

Another specialty of Sicily, as foods go, is the kind of coffee. First, the coffee beans, as in all regions of Italy, are roasted until they are almost charred, ground, then run through a contraption called an "espresso" machine. And when one is dining out, the espresso is usually taken at the bar of the restaurant. The coffee or "espresso" machine is a mixture of valves, pipes, dials, and gauges, doubtless patterned after the boiler room of Fulton's Folly; and after an appropriate amount of coughing, huffing, puffing, and spitting, the machine grudgingly gives up a thimblefull of coffee that you could put in your eye. But don't! It is stronger than moonshine, black as tar, and just as tasty. The natives love it.

Pasta, in its various forms and under its various sauces, together with espresso coffee, are two of the staples of which Sicilians seem never to tire. They are constantly guzzling, storing away these two staples of diet at various hours of the day or night.

During the winter of 1933, I did a large part of my opera work in the two largest cities of Sicily, Palermo and Catania, and in four performances of *Madama Butterfly* and thirteen of *Adriana Lecouvreur*. Each opera has two protagonists because the title role is so difficult (blame composer Cilèa). For the Puccini opus, we had sopranos Rosetta Pampanini and Mafalda Favero, and for *Adriana Lecouvreur*, Giuseppina

Cobelli and Adelaide Saraceni. Not only was each noted for the opera she was to interpret, but each of these sopranos was also among the most handsome women of Italy. Opera-goers truly got the worth of their money during those far-off Sicilian opera seasons. I had just come south from doing an oratorio in Switzerland and had noticed, even in the stretch of so little as one mile, that you knew you were in Italy when the ordered, manicured countryside became sloppy, littered, homey, and lived-in.

Palermo is Sicily's largest city, Catania its second. Catania lies in the shadow of the volcano, Mount Etna, and is subject constantly to its whims. Etna is approximately 10,700 feet high and covers a total of about 500 square miles around its base. There have been more than 136 recorded eruptions since the eighth century B.C., with one as recent as 1971. The warm temperature and the lush soil grow orange, lemon, crabapple, and olive trees, most of which were destroyed, along with the entire city of Catania itself, in the historic eruption of Etna in 1166 A.D., one of the worst earthquake tragedies in history. In Palermo, the Teatro Massimo, with its huge stage, is one of the opera houses most noted in Europe. Catania's Teatro Bellini was built from the plans of the architect Sada who built LaScala.

The composer Bellini was a native of Catania, and his remains are buried in the wall of the city's Cathedral. Looking up toward the mountains, one feels the pull of Eternity and the meaninglessness of Time, also the insignificance of man. There were times, in both Palermo and Catania, when I was practically commuting between the two cities to fulfill the demands of my contract to sing in both cities during the same period of time.

The cab drivers of Palermo are a special breed. There is no

member of the Mafia more a brigand than the city's cabbies. Their rates are high to begin with, and there are "extra" charges for extra passengers and pieces of luggage. Anything that won't fit into your pocket automatically becomes a valise. (How well I know!) Once during the opera season in Palermo, and later in Catania, I had three days of respite when I had no performance and no rehearsals. Together with a sweet young contralto from Lombardy, in whom I was quite interested that winter, a blonde, by the way, along with my long-time friends, Melchiorre Luise and his wife Tina, we hired a car (a Lancia) by the day and set out to visit certain points of interest.

We found Agrigento completely interesting as regards its historical background. Too, Agrigento is world famous for its fine wines, principally muscatel. And during our drives through the environs of Palermo itself, the mosaics at Monreale we found most unbelievable. The walls are literally covered with miles of mosaics and all of them are pleasing, every design different. In the neighborhood of Catania, we were especially taken with the beauties of Taormina. The town stands some four hundred feet above the sea and is a winter refuge both chic and secluded. From the Greco-Roman open air theatre where spectacles are performed in season, you can look up to the snowfields of Mount Etna and down to the beach of Mazzaro. All is so scenic, so "right"— "where every prospect pleases and only man is vile."

During one of our opera performances, there had been a noisy earthquake with corresponding eruptions from Mount Etna, so with transportation at our command, we drove in the direction of the wall of smoke which the wind kept blowing toward the city. And occasionally there would be a blast of hot wind heavily laden with chemical smells which brought

SICILIAN INTERLUDE

on heavy coughing. Our driver took us to within a few miles of the actual crater. We might have gone further, but a river of lava suddenly barred our way. It was traveling downhill very slowly, but when it overcame a tree, there was a flash of flame as the white melted rock encompassed the tree and melted it into nothingness almost instantly.

Adriana Lecouvreur was new to the Sicilians, but they loved it and its tuneful music instantly. Some of my happiest memories are associated with this opera in the Bellini Theatre of Catania. Lines of "stage-door Johnnies" awaited our nightly leaving the theatre, and I can still hear the chant of our names which these "fans and fannies" concocted. It was such an inspiration to work with the finest interpreters of this opera. When the Metropolitan in New York, a few years back, brought out *Adriana Lecouvreur* as a novelty on their year's program, the noted performers who did so splendidly at LaScala, in Catania, and elsewhere in Europe, were no longer living. What a shame it is that today's generation cannot see, feel, and be a part of the great tonal art that belonged to the noted interpreters of a few years back. (Them wuz the days!)

The Cycle

Spring is a hope,
Summer's a song,
Autumn's a dream
Ere Winter, long.

Winter's a sleep
Waiting the May;
Thus do the years
Hasten away.

Up One Minute, Down the Next

The noted conductor at the turn of the century, Walter Damrosch, was also a composer of some note. He added much to the glitter of the trio of men of that illustrious family whose name is cut deep into the advancement of American music during those years, years which today seem so far away. He wrote the baritone's "prize song" *Danny Deever*. It is a sure-fire success even when done with the talents of a poor singer. When done by a good singer with a theatrical flare, it is truly a "prize song." The inordinate success of *Danny Deever* was due to Rudyard Kipling's stirring words and Damrosch's equally stirring music. The Damrosch talent, however, presses far beyond the oomp-ta-ta of sheet-music singing, for he also wrote instrumental solos and orchestral devices of haunting beauty.

Damrosch's musical background was exceptionally rich, for aside from orchestral and choral compositions, as conductor he did the first performances in the United States of Brahms' Third and Fourth Symphonies, *Tapiola* by Sibelius,

Tchaikovsky's Fourth and Sixth Symphonies, and others. Deeply dyed by the colors of Wagner, he managed to adapt chordal progressions to a nice line in some, if not in all, of his lyric operas. Among the operas which Walter Damrosch wrote are: *The Scarlet Letter* (after Hawthorne), *Cyrano de Bergerac, The Man Without a Country, The Opera Cloak,* and *The Dove of Peace.* Mr. Damrosch was also active in radio, his classical orchestra concerts being featured on the Educational Radio Network, and on November 15, 1926, he conducted the first-ever chain broadcast over the newly organized NBC network.

It was on May 12, 1937, that Mr. Damrosch's opera, *Man Without a Country*, was given its first airing. Its premiere was at the Metropolitan Opera and with a carefully selected cast, each role occupied by a stellar name. But there had been too few rehearsals, and no one on stage was too sure of himself. The lack of proper rehearsing was due to strikes among the electrical unions which had spread also to the group of movers, members of the AFL-CIO who transported all stage scenery round-trip between backstage at the Met and the storage barns on Staten Island. This having the stage and its sets separated and having to have the scenery for every individual production brought by truck was one of the most frustrating and far too frequent occurrences for the peace of mind of all concerned. We had heard by backstage grapevine that so ill prepared were the members of the cast for the new opera that it would have to be canceled, since postponing when a season's agenda is already full is impossible. Mr. Damrosch, however, gave the cast a pep talk, and it was voted to go ahead as originally planned.

Since she is today quite active in things musical in the New York area, it would be hardly fair to use the real name of the young woman who was singing a lead soprano role in this new opera, so I shall refer to her as Miss X.

The time of *Man Without a Country* is the Colonial Period of American history, and that, for the ladies in the cast, meant semi-hoopskirts. All of the costumes were naturally brand new, so very new, in fact, that one never knew where to find the proper button or the too-small hole in the leather belt. There had been only a walk-through rehearsal after the costumes became available, and that was overly hurried and was held not even on the Met's stage, but upstairs in the ballet rehearsal room. (Those days in the old opera house at 39th and Broadway could be heavy with worries as well as thrilling when things went well.)

Miss X had a fetching costume in Act I. I recall that it was red handloomed wool with black raised squares shadowed in off-white. Her square-toed black hand-rubbed shoes with square heels and a wide leather belt made for a fetching ensemble.

It was not a sold-out house, so it was possible for some of us to get gratis passes for the artists' box. I was one of the fortunate ones. After all, being present at a world premiere is not possible very often. One soon became aware that this opera's music was written by a devotee of Richard Wagner: constantly "promising" a melody but seldom fulfilling that promise.

Miss X had just finished one of these rather unmelodic passages when, as she turned to run up a short stairway to a garden terrace, as the score demanded, suddenly down came her unmentionables and there they lay in full view of all sections of the audience. Later on, Miss X said that they dropped without warning; but even so, what is one supposed to do in such a case? She did something so graceful that many did not realize what had taken place. Delaying her exit up the garden steps, she caused the audience to believe that she was going offstage through a right side door. In the brief moment needed for this byplay, she kicked the offending lingerie into the wings and then ran up the garden steps as though nothing had occurred. It was a touchy problem neatly solved and so gracefully maneuvered, that since it was a new opera, many thought this was in the story and a part of Miss X's interpretation. Years have passed but Miss X is still kidded about the night she lost her you-know-whats.

First Plane Ride

Each of us remembers his first airplane ride. During the 1920's, short rides in planes were sometimes awarded as prizes at county fairs and at out-of-door conventions where the unusual or even the bizarre was wanted. Once I had the chance for such a test run when our Sooner Trio was appearing before the State Convention of Oklahoma Bankers. (The other two members of the Trio had taken the reckless ride, but I had not, nor did I, fearing the worst.) From September of 1923 to October of 1935, I sang in opera in Europe, and with all respect to their brilliance in many fields, Europeans never did much toward commercializing air travel, proving themselves to be better followers of the USA's initiative than pioneers in air travel themselves. It was Lindbergh's solo flight across the Atlantic in 1927 that opened up the market for air travel for and by Europeans. In Milan, Italy, when a student there, I used to watch an occasional passenger plane glide gracefully over the enormity of the Alps and wonder what the sensation would be like to be an integral part *of* that sensation. I was soon to find out. It happened as follows.

On November 13, 1934, I had made my opera debut in my native land. The vehicle was Puccini's *Tosca* at the Chicago opera, and the cast was a stellar one: Maria Jeritza as Tosca, Pasquale Amato as Scarpia, myself as Mario Cavaradossi, and Maestro Gennaro Papi, directing. The National Broadcasting Company (NBC) in New York was looking for suitable casts for the "Opera in English" radio hour for Chase and Sanborn Coffee Company which was coming up soon as a replacement for the enormously popular Eddie Cantor-Rubinoff program, 8:00 to 9:00 P.M. on Sundays. They needed a tenor. Scouts for NBC in Chicago had heard and seemed to like my singing in *Tosca*, so through my agent they signed me for thirteen weeks. The new hour was to emanate from New York and was to start December 2 with *Rigoletto* (with John Charles Thomas, Josephine Antoine, and me). The drawback was that I had a contract with the Chicago opera where manager Paul Longone was rightfully jealous of his singers. He scowled woefully when I told him of my contract with NBC. I was booked to sing in the matinee of *Madama Butterfly* in Chicago the preceding afternoon, December 1. Too, our one-and-only rehearsal with the new English translation was to be at 9:30 A.M. the morning of the day of the broadcast which was to be that night. To do it honorably and on time required flying from Chicago to New York. But! For eleven days all of the Chicago area had been covered with ice up to four inches thick and no planes had taken off from any of the several neighboring airstrips around Chicago, although a few desperate landings had been permitted. There had been no melting weather, but the runways had been sanded well and the commercial lines were hoping to re-establish skeleton service.

In *Madama Butterfly*, it is the tenor who sings the first and final notes of the opera. I had told the title-role singer, soprano Edith Mason, of my hurried plans (although the Chicago press had played them up even on the front page of certain editions), and that after one curtain call at the end of the opera with her and the others I would leave. This was done, and I joined the motorcycle-police squad which the opera house's management had kindly gotten to help get me to the airport (also for reasons of good publicity). Away we rushed, police sirens chilling the icy air still more. It was eighteen miles from Chicago's Loop to the old airport. We made it in less time than permitted by law.

Knowing that it would be necessary for me to go to the airport without changing costume and with stage make-up still on, I had brought along a tube of theatrical cold cream and some tissue, but in the excitement of events all happening at once, instead of removing grease paint, I began removing pants. Now, did you ever try to change pants when seated in the middle of a limousine's back seat with an opera publicity man on one side of you and a policeman on the other, not to mention your valise riding on your feet? Also, can you imagine the looks on the faces of the other airline passengers when they beheld this Phantom of the Opera arriving in such condition? (The plane had been held twenty-two minutes.) Press photos flashed, and my verbal thanks were said to the chauffeur and the police escort who had gotten me to the airport in such record time.

The stewardess showed me to my seat, and soon we had taxied to the far end of the recently sanded runway. In short the new abundance of sand atop the old ice caused the wheels to spin. We got off the ground, but after only a few feet in the air nose-dived to the earth, twisting the propellers into bizarre shapes. Fortunately there was no fire, no one was hurt, nor did the plane turn over. Some three hours later, and in a different plane, we again took off. At once I went to the washroom and removed all make-up possible and changed to civilian clothes. The plane touched down at Detroit and Pittsburgh without incident and shortly, east of Pittsburgh, ran completely out of the storm clouds and into a beautifully serene night sky. My emotions followed suit and soared with patriotic pride as we circled Manhattan Island with its myriad of lights as we prepared to land at Newark Airport. That night's memory of seeing New York's high-rise buildings from above, rather than in or beside them, is ever fresh in my mind, and although I have flown many thousands of miles since then, no trip by air can rival my first one.

Opera in English Radio Hour

NBC's "Opera in English" radio hour of 1935–36 was a proud combination since everything about it was stellar. Our opening broadcast was of *Rigoletto*, a smash hit, about which we received bags of fan mail, most of it commendatory, yet with a few thistles among the eider down. One evidently elderly Italian woman wrote us, in Italian, that it was a spiritual "sin" to try to graft "the impossible English language upon the waving beauty of Verdi's rich harmonies." Another, probably a native of the USA and certainly a man because of his bold handwriting, asked how *The Star-Spangled Banner* would sound sung in Italian. So, he avowed, he was "stricken" by the ineptitude of hearing the charm of Italian vowels replaced by the windmill clatter of English's "too numerous consonants." Rather a strong comment, this, but partly true, we must admit.

The "Opera in English" series of twenty-six radio broadcasts was held in Studio 8-H Radio City's RCA Building and before a live audience of some fifteen hundred. So great was the demand for those gratis tickets that policemen had to take over on two occasions. One hundred and nine radio stations carried these condensed opera programs, and the press estimated that several million people listened each sunday evening. Every opera was trimmed to fit the allotted time of each broadcast by a committee made up of Deems Taylor, Maestro Wilfred Pelletier, directing the NBC Symphony Orchestra, and two executive secretaries from the national office for radio. And, so that the most would be had from the title of the program, Miss Madeleine Marshall, head diction coach at the Juilliard School of Music, had been employed to make a completely new translation of the original text, and to be present and offer suggestions at all rehearsals for each opera of the series.

In the first thirteen weeks' broadcasting of the eventual total of twenty-six weeks, I did five operas. They were *Rigoletto, Tales of Hoffmann, Madama Butterfly, Carmen,* and Massenet's *Manon*. Others taking leading roles were John Charles Thomas, Elizabeth Rethberg, Grete Stueckgold, Lucrezia Bori, Josephine Antoine, Hilda Burke, Lawrence Tibbett, and others. The opulent days of radio!

Erna Sack

Chicago is a town that loves things bizarre, sensational, and superlative. During the 1930's, the manager of the Opera of Chicago, Paul Longone, was a man after Chicago's own heart, because he also loved these same things and did what he could to supply the city's adolescent yearnings, even to changing the name of the dignified "Opera of Chicago" to "The Chicago City Opera."

Longone visited Europe during the summer of 1935, and at Salzburg heard Erna Sack for the first time. Her coloratura singing was quite remarkable, but like a stellar acrobatic act in a circus, unsatisfying; and, without the support of the German text, her singing was vapid, monotonous, and dull; however, Longone signed her up for single performances of *Rigoletto*, *Barber of Seville*, and *Traviata*, deciding to whet the desire of Chicago ticket buyers by advertising her as the woman who could sing the highest notes in the world. For, as is known all over everywhere to most Americans, the best singer is the one who sings the highest.

Up to now, all well and good. Frau Sack was to make her first operatic appearance in Chicago as Gilda in *Rigoletto* on November 16, 1935. She and her baron-husband arrived the previous week with her three operas for Chicago all polished, but in the German language only!

Now, John Charles Thomas, the noted American baritone, was doing his first *Rigoletto*, except for the baritone's arias and the Garden Scene duet with the soprano, which he had performed on his radio programs. So, he was depending on the question in Italian before he could give the answer in kind. The rehearsals were completely unpleasant since it was difficult to communicate with the German soprano, who understood conversation only in her native language. During the final rehearsal with the orchestra, and after an especially trying scene, John Charles said in a loud voice, "Joe, what in the . . . is she jabbering at me?!!" (I had wondered, too).

Came the performance. In the beautiful soprano and tenor duet, *"E'il sol dell'anima,"* toward the end, all at once Frau Sack suddenly began to sing her part an octive higher and all phrases fortissimo (later on she said that such was to cause "interest"). She mangled *"Caro nome"* until not even Verdi would have recognized it. Somehow we got through *Rigoletto* that night, but Frau Sack and her Baron left Chicago the following day, and other sopranos sang her *Barber of Seville* and *Traviata*. Contrary to what Longone had hoped for in Salzburg, no one had a good word for Frau Sack in Chicago. We all had suffered when she tried to show off her own vocal talents. She never sang again with the Opera of Chicago.

The Protested Tenor

Some thirty-odd kilometers by highway southeast of Milan, and on the road to Cremona, is the community of Codogno, noted for the manufacturing and packaging of Parmesan cheese, the shipping of wheat, ceramics, and the love of opera. The town is prosperous since there is a pride in the work of each profession. Too, many of the city's families are interrelated.

November 20, 1932, was a date filled with excited activity for me. Returning to my Milan hotel, Il Vecchio Cervo (The Old Deer), I found that my agent and several head operators of the telephone company had been trying in vain to contact me by telephone. The hotel manager said that a noted Italian tenor had been protested by the public of Codogno the preceding night in Puccini's opera, *Manon Lescaut*, and would I come and sing the second performance that very night? They would have called sooner, they said, but they were trying to patch things up with the protested tenor, however in vain.

The soprano singing the title role at Codogno was Rosetta Pampanini, one of the greatest interpreters of that opera. She had been the choice of Arturo Toscanini for that role when he had visited Germany with certain productions from La-Scala, Puccini's *Manon Lescaut* one of them. She had recommended me at Codogno. I telephoned the management at Codogno that I would come by livery-taxi to save time. So with my two valises of costumes and make-up in the trunk of the car, my agent, his assistant, and me in the car, we were off for Codogno. The manager had said on the telephone that he would hold the spectacle until we could get there. All the way, however, I kept wondering if I, a foreigner, had made the right decision about stepping into such a ticklish position. But all such doubts were dissolved when we rounded the Piazza dell'Unita. The square was almost filled with people, waiting to buy tickets, and for our arrival. It was then 9:20 P.M. I greeted Rosetta Pampanini and briefly compared some tricky tempi of Act I with Maestro Cremignani, the conductor, put on my costume for Act I, and at 9:40 P.M. we began the opera. It went well, and the full house gave each of us a round of applause as we appeared and at the end of each act. Three more performances were done during the coming week, each a success, but none as exciting as that one following the hectic ride from Milan.

Diplomatic Dinner

The first part of 1938 brought me two appearances in Washington, D.C. The first one was on January 13, in the form of a joint recital with Rose Bampton, soprano, and Catherine Littlefield, ballerina, following the annual Diplomatic Dinner in the East Room of the White House. The second appearance was on April 25, when my accompanist from the University of Oklahoma, Merl Freeland, and I gave the entire program of eleven songs in the Mayflower Hotel Ballroom following the Congressional Club's annual breakfast honoring Mrs. Eleanor Roosevelt. Neither of these programs was a "thank you" appearance, but was contracted and paid for like any other commercial concert.

The annual Diplomatic Dinner is one of the most festive events of the social year in Washington, D.C., so we were told, and I can easily believe it. To this dinner is invited a certain number of the upper crust of diplomats serving every nation with which our country has diplomatic relations. Since it is traditional for men to wear dressy military or other uniforms to this dinner, such makes a fine excuse for their women to try to outdo each other in regality of evening gowns. The result is completely colorful. With the exception of the United Nations, it is doubtful if anywhere on earth is there such a concentrated show of lavishness based upon what these selected representatives of the various countries consider good taste in gala clothing.

Since this was the Diplomatic Dinner and French is the language of diplomacy, I selected for my part of the program, aside from three Old English songs, a brace of classical French songs by Messager, Fourdrain, and Charpentier (the tenor aria from his opera *Louise*). Miss Bampton emphasized German *Lieder*. We closed the program with the duet from the first act of *Madama Butterfly*. Miss Littlefield danced to music by Tchaikovsky.

The large ballroom was full, and following the program, there were many to greet, several of them from Oklahoma.

Iphigenia in Aulis

Because it is so complicated to stage, Gluck's opera *Iphigenia in Aulis* until 1935 had never been given in the United States. Based upon the adaptation of a play by Racine, there is almost as much for ballet in this opera as there is singing, and several times, as the opera progresses and the orchestra plays on, quick changes of groups on the stage have to be made within the space of only a few seconds—ballet on, chorus off, and so on. The Philadelphia Orchestra, for some years, had wanted to present this masterpiece of Gluck's on the orchestra's season ticket. Finally, in February of 1935, it became a possibility. Since the original text was French, we sang the opera in that language. "We" included soprano Rosa Tentoni in the title role, Cyrena van Gordon, mezzo, as Clytemnestra, Georges Baklanov as Agamemnon, and myself as Achilles, the Philadelphia Orchestra and Chorus under the leadership of Maestro Alexander Smallens.

Doing the honors for the many ballets in the score were the Humphrey-Weidman Dancers. The entire production was under the supervision of Norman Bel Geddes and Herbert Graf, who used spotlights of various colors instead of scenery, and sometimes combined them with stairwells of pure light to achieve novel effects—Hollywoodish, yes, but dramatic and pleasingly different, too. Costuming, too, was original. For example, my first costume and helmet were Grecian military ones of gilded smooth goatskin ornamented with suede leather of a darker gold color. The second costume was the same one, but with an added military cape of soft gray wool which caught the colored spotlights in a fetching manner.

This opera was given originally in Paris in 1774, so having its first American performance 161 years later created comment and publicity in music circles the country over. It was fun having an active part in such a happy event in music.

Will Rogers

Will Rogers was an American favorite, even of those whose type of person he rightfully lampooned. He was a humorist, an actor, a writer, and most of all, a staunch Oklahoman. The column he wrote each weekday filled with that good common (Okie) sense brought many a refreshing shower of emotion. Will was a master at deflating the pompous, of pricking a tight balloon filled with imagined self-importance, at reducing the "would-be's" to the "has-been's." The American enjoyment of fair play responded wholeheartedly to such treatment and loved Will for it.

Will Rogers and the noted Oklahoma aviator Wiley Post were killed near Point Barrow, Alaska, August 15, 1935, when their plane fell. That summer I was getting needed stage experience by appearing as Dr. Valenti in *Men in White* with the Stockbridge Players, and I remember hearing over the radio in the automobile in which I was a passenger of the tragic death of these two noted men.

Each state is allowed by law to have two representatives in

the National Hall of Fame in the Rotunda of the National Capitol in Washington, D.C. Oklahoma, already represented by Sequoyah, chose Will Rogers to be the second. (Oklahoma is thus represented by two Cherokees, for Will was part Cherokee.) By 1939, with funds available, Jo Davidson sculptured a bronze statue in slightly larger-than-life proportions, and on June 6, 1939, the statue was dedicated. Governor Leon Phillips and Luther Harrison, Editor of the Oklahoma City *Times*, spoke, the Marine Band played, and I sang, using, in addition to Malotte's setting of "The Lord's Prayer," Geoffrey O'Hara's fine song to Longfellow's poem "Good Will to Men."

Good Will to Men

"Good will to men," I heard one day
From out a manger far away,
And wild and sweet the words repeat
Of peace on earth, good will to men.

> *And thought how, as the day had come,*
> *The belfries of all Christendom*
> *Had rolled along the unbroken song*
> *Of peace on earth, good will to men.*

>> *Then came the war with flags unfurled*
>> *And cannon thundered through the world*
>> *And with the sound the gladness drowned*
>> *Of peace on earth, good will to men.*

It was as if an earthquake rent
The hearth-stones of a continent,
And made forlorn the households born
Of peace on earth, good will to men.

Then in despair I bowed my head;
"There is no peace on earth," I said,
"For hate is strong and mocks the song
Of peace on earth, good will to men."

   Then pealed the bells more loud and deep
   "God is not dead nor does He sleep.
   The Wrong shall fail, the Right prevail,
   With peace on earth, good will to men."

Henry Wadsworth Longfellow

Although written during the heat of the War Between the States, the focus of this poem is quite applicable to world conditions today. It strikes a basic response in the heart of each of us, including that of this "Oklahoma Tenor."

Why

*Why do I sing such foolish songs
That are bald of rhythm and worth,
Songs that mean so little
And are common as mother-earth?*

*Songs with no glint of meaning,
No style, no direction, no rhyme,
That seem a waste of energy
And certainly a waste of time.*

*Why do I write such foolish songs
That are worthless and common as dust?
Simply for the reason
That I must.*